CONNECTING PEOPLE
CREATING ENGAGING ENVIRONMENTS

KATE DAVIES

First published in Great Britain in 2015
by LEC Connect Ltd

Copyright © Kate Davies

The author's rights are fully asserted. The right of Kate Davies to be identified as the author of this work has been asserted by her in accordance with the Copyright, Designs and Patents Act 1988.

All rights reserved; no part of this publication may be reproduced, stored in a retrieval system, or transmitted in any form or by any means, electronic, mechanical, photocopying, recording or otherwise, without the prior permission of the publisher. Nor be circulated in any form of binding or cover other than that in which it is published and a similar condition including this condition being imposed on the subsequent purchaser.

A CIP Catalogue of this book is available from the British Library.

ISBN: 978-0-9932174-0-1 (paperback)

Also available as an ebook
First published as an ebook in 2015

ISBN: 978-0-9932174-1-8 (Mobi)
ISBN: 978-0-9932174-2-5 (epub)

Cover design and typeset by
www.chandlerbookdesign.co.uk

Printed in Great Britain by
PrintonDemand-Worldwide

What's in the book?

Who is this book for? — 1

1. Engagement on two pages — 3
2. Why bother? — 5
   Why do this? — 6
3. What is engagement? — 9
   How does it feel? — 9
   How do engaged and disengaged people behave? — 11
4. What helps people engage? — 19
   Purpose — 21
   Capability — 23
   Control — 24
5. What happens when we put these things together? — 27
6. What can I do about engagement? — 35
7. Plot the journey — 39
   Why is this important? — 39
   Gather the data — 41
   Surveys – uses and abuses — 43
   Parent-child contract — 43
   Paint-the-walls-a-different colour syndrome — 46
   Engagement in isolation — 48
   To survey or not to survey? — 52
   Interpret the data — 53
   Identify the way ahead — 55
   Create your statement of intent — 58
8. Connect with people — 63
   Share the purpose — 63
   Make the purpose relevant — 64

Crafting the message	64
What's it got to do with me?	66
Keep going: say it, be it	71
Say it once, say it twice, then say it again	71
Be it	71

9. Involve people — 75

Brilliant managers	76
You	78
Inspiring, trusted, authentic communicator of the 'why'	80
Creator of opportunities	84
Proficient operator	87
Celebrator of progress	89
Culture builder	91
Capable people	94
You as a strategic leader of the business	94
You as a developer of people	97
Owning my own development	100
Exercising freedom	102

10. Some specific applications — 107

Taking people with you through change	108
Developing effective virtual teams	118
Building profitable, long-lasting customer relationships	127

11. What do you do next? — 133

Appendix: Case Studies	135
Appendix: MAP tool	143
Appendix: HIC tool– Help, Impact, Control	145
Appendix: Gap Analysis	147
Reading list	149
A bit about Kate Davies	151

This book is dedicated to the lovely Ralph who has brought sense to my meanderings and supported when I have doubted.

It is also dedicated to the many people and teams I have worked with – in particular Jenny Munn who held me to high account, Matt Jeans, a genius with people, Roger Hodson who showed me the meaning of bravery, Malcolm Parker, my invaluable first mentor on 'engagement' and Gavin Rogerson, who put his faith in me and taught me the meaning of leadership through his own outstanding example.

I would also like to thank the people who contributed directly to this book with their thoughts and insights. In particular, Amanda Cooke, Jackie Ducker, Liz Ellis, Julie Goodwin, the team at K2, Deni Lyall, Mary Zacaroli and my BRAC Consulting colleagues – Sabina Mangosi and Mark Davies. And of course thanks to the many other anonymous contributors, colleagues, writers and lecturers who have influenced, broadened and deepened my thinking – I hope I have shown my gratitude by making good use of their ideas and developing them further.

Who is this book for?

Connecting People is primarily written for the person I was some years ago – a new line manager, facing the responsibilities of developing her team, and given a goal of 'improving engagement'. I had no idea what 'engagement' meant or what I was supposed to do about it. I learnt from my mentor and the people around me, and gradually developed my skills and own style of leading and engaging. However, I might have avoided some of the mistakes I made, or found a quicker route through, if this book had been available. So if you are a new line manager, or struggling with a team that's not as engaged as they could be, this book is for you.

Of course more seasoned managers and executives may also find parts of this book useful, perhaps because it might remind you about what less experienced line managers face or because some of the content is pertinent to all leaders.

What can you expect from this book?

The book is a manual for people who want to know how they can create environments that encourage people to participate to the full extent of their abilities. It uses and references some models to help frame your thinking, and gives practical tips on how to apply them with your teams. It also has some exercises to help you think through the ideas presented and make them relevant to your own situation.

It is not an academic book, drawing on data from a large, statistically valid survey. I have used references to people and organisations where I think this helps to illustrate a point, but the content of the book is mainly derived from my experiences as a leader in a business, my observations of other teams I have worked with, and the many conversations I have had with colleagues, friends, associates and others who are passionate about engagement.

This book doesn't have all the answers, but it does have some.

1
Engagement on two pages

Engagement is about making a personal choice to participate to the full extent of my abilities, to achieve something I value, and doing this consistently as a matter of course.

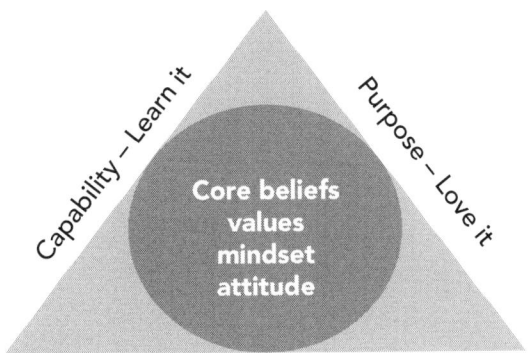

When I'm fully engaged, there is a far higher likelihood that I will achieve what I set out to achieve.

This momentum multiplies when we bring engaged people together in teams. When I'm engaged and the people around me act in the same way, we become formidable in what we can do. With this dynamic, we greatly increase the likelihood of both our team and the organisation we work for achieving what it sets out to achieve.

For a leader in a business, it is about creating an environment in which people make this choice more consistently and more of the time. Leaders can achieve this by plotting the journey, connecting with people and involving them.

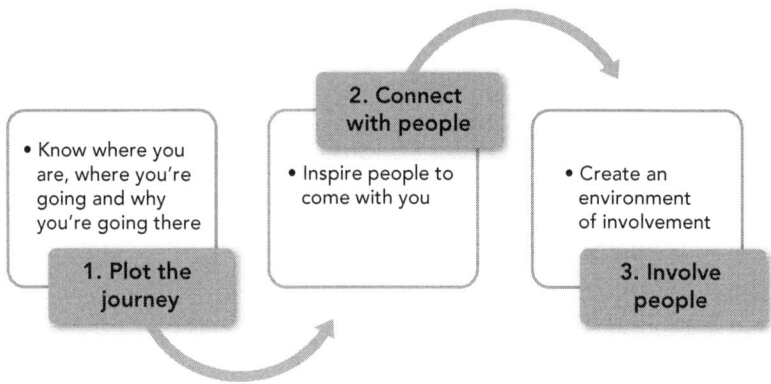

If you get this right, you create an environment in which everyone - the individual, the teams they work in and the organisation they work for - is pulling in the same direction. If you choose not to bother, you are choosing to operate with at least one arm (and possibly all four limbs) tied behind your back – at best an uncomfortable position.

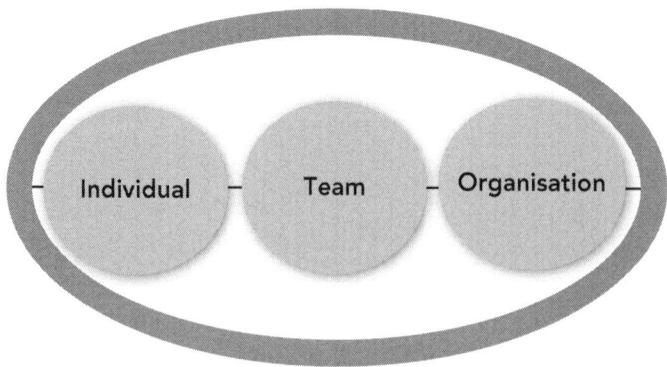

2

Why bother?

> *"I'm working hard, meeting my targets, managing my team, minding my own business. What's engagement got to do with me?"*

I admit to thinking this exact thought when my boss first told me to "do something about engagement" in my new team. Things were ticking along okay; we were getting the product out to customers and meeting our deadlines. The only problem was the team had a low engagement score – whatever that was – and my boss wanted me to improve it.

There is a section on 'Engagement Surveys and Scores' later in the book. Suffice to say here that the low engagement score had the effect of focusing my mind – not least because part of my bonus was tied to this goal – and I got on with working out how to create a more engaged team.

Although that was my experience at the time, I would like to start you off from a different place. It is not about raising a score on a survey. It is about nurturing the enthusiasm, creativeness, energy and tenacity of your team and helping them to put it to good use.

Why do this?

There are many motivations that will influence you. You may be driven by a desire to make people happy or enjoy developing people. You may strive to achieve stretched goals and know that you need a high-performing team around you to achieve them. You may enjoy the accolade that goes with leading a great team, or the promise of a good bonus may be all it takes.

I can't second-guess your motivations but I can look at it from a very basic level: you are a manager, and your team are your resource. If your laptop was only working 80% of the time, you would be throwing it at the IT team and demanding they fix it. Why would you think it's okay that your team is anything less than 100% engaged in what they are doing?

If your internal motivations haven't yet convinced you and the IT analogy doesn't get you going, take a look at the research conducted by the Engage for Success group[1]. This group, which brings together engagement practitioners and gurus from across the UK, has shown that organisations (big, small, public sector, private sector, utilities to retail and services) that have highly engaged staff do better on a whole range of measures.

Profits and revenue growth are twice as high in these organisations than in competitors. Customers are 12% more satisfied. Employees are far more innovative, productive and efficient; they have better health and safety records; and staff turnover is 40% lower. All these outcomes are good for your business and they come with higher levels of engagement.

We can sum this up by saying highly engaged staff increase the likelihood of an organisation achieving what it sets out to achieve.

But I would add a note of caution.

---

[1] Engage for Success: www.engageforsuccess.org

A company I work with, K2, are passionate about human performance, and their opening gambit is that 'Talent is Not Enough'[2]. Similarly, I would argue that a desire to engage is not enough. It is how that engagement translates into behaviours that matters, and whether the people in the organisation have truly created an environment that nurtures and channels this engagement to greatest effect that truly makes the difference.

The next chapter looks at this in more detail but just in case you are not yet persuaded that 'engagement' and unleashing its power is something you should be bothered about, I will end this chapter with a cautionary tale about what happens when engagement is absent or, as in this case, stifled.[3]

The Mid-Staffordshire NHS Foundation Trust

'Cautionary tale' makes it sound as though this comes from the fairy stories of the Brothers Grimm. Unfortunately, this tale is very real and relates to the catastrophic events that put the Stafford Hospital and the Mid-Staffordshire NHS Foundation Trust into the headlines for all the wrong reasons, with people dying who shouldn't have.

> *NHS hospital scandal which left 1,200 dead could happen again, warn campaigners - Daily Mail*

> *NHS trust's litany of failure, neglect, insensitivity and ineptitude - The Guardian*

> *Hospital condemned over deaths after 'appalling' failures in care - The Guardian*

An easy conclusion to jump to was that the culture in the NHS had gone wrong; that somehow the staff had stopped caring for their

---

[2] Planet K2: www.planetk2.com

[3] Professor David Buchanan, Professor Mike Bourne, Steve Macaulay, Cranfield University School of Management *"Mid Staffs: making the right decisions"*, Article for *Health Service Journal*, 28 March 2013

patients. Professor David Buchanan, Professor Mike Bourne and Steve Macaulay of Cranfield University looked into this and came to a different conclusion. Their research showed that people working in the NHS were strongly motivated and wanted to make a difference for patients, deliver innovation and change, do a good job, feel valued, and develop others - all characteristics of highly engaged people (see How do engaged and disengaged people behave?).

However, these motivations were stifled by an autocratic, unsupportive, top-down management style, a complex regulatory regime, constant change in structures (requiring people to spend a lot of energy forging new relationships and understand changes in their role), metrics that focussed too narrowly on financial performance and seemed to ignore the 'softer' measures around care, and a significant cost reduction programme. The will was there but the environment wasn't.

3
What is engagement?

Already in some organisations the word 'Engagement' has been consigned to the overuse bin, rejected by the cynics and now only whispered in corridors by the people for whom it still has some meaning…. Feel familiar?

Let me attempt to reclaim its usefulness by setting out what I think it means. At its strongest 'engagement' is a verb: it's about participating, taking part, engaging with something to achieve something. As a noun it is also pretty strong: engagement describes a contract (e.g. between people or to do something specific) and all contracts involve something being given and received by both parties.

This might be what engagement is, but it still doesn't really describe it. Two dimensions that help us here are to look at what engagement feels like, and how we behave when we are highly engaged.

How does it feel?

What does being engaged in something feel like?

Imagine a day when you've been doing an activity you really enjoy. Then ask yourself:

It's been a great day....	
What did you do that you really enjoyed?	
What made it enjoyable?	
How did this day differ from a day when you 'just did your job'?	

At some point I would encourage you to repeat this exercise with your team – it helps people identify their own version of engagement.

This wordle captures some of the things that groups typically come up with when asked these questions.

Figure 1: Description of engagement

Note that the words 'happiness' and 'satisfied' don't appear; nor is the phrase 'earned lots of money'. People do sometimes use these words when asked to describe a situation where they felt highly engaged, but I think they are distractions.

We have to earn a certain amount of money to put a roof over our heads and food in our mouths, and the more money we have, the more choices it gives us. We also generally like to feel happy. These things are necessary to our lives, but not sufficient[4]. Indeed, we could view money and happiness as outcomes of being highly engaged, not the reason we seek to participate in something and give it our all.

The 2012 Olympic Games Makers, and the volunteers at the 2014 Commonwealth Games illustrate this point: thousands of people, of different ages and backgrounds, gave a considerable amount of their free time, to help people attending the Games. They were all unpaid volunteers, working long hours. They were famous for their unstinting enthusiasm and ever-lasting smiles, even late at night after a long day of helping others. While they were clearly happy, that was an outcome of what they did as well as why they did it.

How do engaged and disengaged people behave?

Behaviours are less subjective than feelings. They are also easier for us to observe and do something about – it is very difficult to change a person's feelings about something, but you can set expectations around behaviours and see whether someone is adopting them.

In his book *"The Employee Engagement Mindset"*, Timothy Clark[5] draws on observations and interviews with highly engaged people from a wide variety of backgrounds, cultures, social standing, ages and jobs to identify the characteristics they share. Adding to this work from my own observations, we can potentially identify engaged people as those who:

---

[4] Also see Mihaly Csikszentmihalyi *"Flow: the classic work on how to achieve happiness"*, 2002

[5] Timothy Clark *"The Employee Engagement Mindset"*, 2012

- persevere and seek to achieve
- take ownership (including for their own engagement)
- are accountable for their actions
- collaborate and seek to make a difference
- are curious and dissatisfied
- look for opportunities to learn and improve

These observations chime with the Utrecht University Occupational Psychologists[6] view that:

> 'Engagement is a positive, fulfilling, work-related state of mind that is characterized by vigor, dedication, and absorption. Rather than a momentary and specific state, engagement refers to a more persistent and pervasive affective-cognitive state that is not focused on any particular object, event, individual, or behavior.
>
> Vigor is characterized by high levels of energy and mental resilience while working, the willingness to invest effort in one's work, and persistence even in the face of difficulties. Dedication refers to being strongly involved in one's work and experiencing a sense of significance, enthusiasm, inspiration, pride, and challenge. Absorption, is characterized by being fully concentrated and happily engrossed in one's work, whereby time passes quickly and one has difficulties with detaching oneself from work'.

We can put this understanding to good use as we look for these characteristics within our teams.

---

[6] Utrecht University, Occupational Health Psychology Unit, Wilmar Schaufeli & Arnold Baker *"Work Engagement Scale"*

Matt Jeans, an operations leader at D&B and a natural engager of people, thought it would be useful if line leaders could also identify the characteristics of actively disengaged people. These are people who:

- look for an easy life
- achieve below par, variable results
- don't take ownership and avoid being held accountable
- think the organisation is responsible for keeping them engaged
- resist change and can be disruptive

As a line leader, you are looking to nurture highly engaged behaviours and minimise or eradicate the damaging behaviours of disengaged people. Just take a moment to think about the consequences of not doing these two things. If you don't do the former you are missing out on a powerful resource that will make your business zing. If you don't do the latter, you are wilfully sabotaging your business.

**Two exercises help these lists of attributes come to life.
In the first exercise, think of a couple of people who you think are really engaged:**

Engaged people		
Who are they?	How do they behave?	What effect do they have?

By way of example, we might look at the athletes involved in the 2012 Olympics. There were thousands of people exhibiting huge degrees of engagement (like the Games Makers) but the person who caught my attention was Olympic rower Katherine Grainger. Here was someone who wasn't just highly engaged for the two weeks of the Games, but was highly engaged for her entire rowing career.

The Spanish language makes a distinction between a transitory state of being (estar) and a permanent state of being (ser). Katherine Grainger's dedication to her cause was definitely in the 'ser' category, or the 'persistent and pervasive' state Schaufeli and Baker refer to. Katherine's ambition and level of engagement was a permanent part of her.

I haven't met Katherine, but look at any of the many articles about her and some clear characteristics come out:

- **Dissatisfaction:** Before winning her gold medal in the women's double sculls at the London 2012 Olympic Games, Katherine had already won 6 World Championship gold medals and 3 Olympic silvers, but that wasn't enough: *"You work so hard for gold, silver is a failure"*.
- **Perseverance & focus:** Katherine started her international rowing career in 1997, and rowed in her first Olympic Games in Sydney in 2000. A lot happens during a 15-year international career, but Katherine remained focused and persevered.
- **Belief:** on the morning of her race with Anna Watkins at the 2012 Games, Katherine relates: *"We knew we could do it; we believed it would happen"*.

Once you start looking, you can find engagement (of the permanent 'ser' type) in many places.

In an interview in September 2014 the CEO of the insurer, Lloyds of London, Inga Beale, put much of the 21% rise in profits in the first half of the year down to the expert underwriters at Lloyds, who are not only skilled in pricing risk but are innovative in helping companies and individuals cover new forms of risk, such as cyber attack and reputational damage. I have no idea what the engagement scores would look like at Lloyds of London, but the outcome certainly points to a high level of 'ser' type participation.

Closer to home, we were recently trying to find out what part our daughter's car needed – the car and daughter were in Australia, we were in the UK. A very helpful parts-mechanic in a garage under the Heathrow flight path helped to diagnose what was needed from the paltry information we were able to provide, and let us know other problems that particular make of car was likely to suffer from. If you are thinking this advice was inspired by a desire to sell us something, you would be wrong: he recommended a no-cost remedy to the problem. He took pride in what he was doing and could imagine being a worried parent.

I find it harder to give you examples of disengagement. It is not easy to find them in the public arena (almost by definition people in the public arena are there because they are engaged in something). Disengagement, as with engagement, is also often transitory and specific to a particular activity:

Slow day at the pumps

You pull up to a petrol pump and step out of your nice warm car and briefly shiver as the cold, wet evening wraps around you. And you wait… Eventually, someone, somewhere (in a nice, warm kiosk) presses a reset button and you can start using the pump.

You fill up and go into the kiosk to pay. And you wait… Two people are behind their cash desk, chatting about the football match that was on the telly last night. They are highly engaged in this conversation and very skilled at avoiding all eye contact with the three people waiting in a queue to pay.

You finally get to the head of the queue. And you wait… A delivery person has just arrived and the person who was just about to process your payment has leapt out of their chair to deal with it…

The two people 'serving' were clearly engaged in lots of activity that evening, but possibly not engaged in what you might consider to be their main role of taking your payment quickly and accurately.

In the second exercise, think of a couple of people who you think are really disengaged:

Disengaged people		
Who are they?	What do you notice about how they behave?	What effect do they have?

As a quick guide, we might identify passively disengaged people as the ones you get poor service from, they are the ones who simply don't care what effect they have on you. They probably don't get up in the morning thinking "I'm going to do a really bad job today", but equally, they're not interested in the job you need them to do.

Symptoms might be an upswing in staff attrition or a downswing in discretionary effort. One company I interviewed for this book noticed that their staff were working far fewer hours as the organisation went through a period of sizeable change. Where people had routinely been working 50 plus hours a week, they were now working the bare minimum, not out of belligerency but because they were feeling uncertain about their futures.

Actively disengaged people are people who set out to undermine the efforts of others. Fortunately I haven't come across many people like this. Rather than speculate about why some people act in this way, my focus with these individuals has usually been to reflect back to them the effect they are having and give them a choice – desist and change, or move on to something they can engage with.

It is not as stark as it sounds. These conversations often take place over a period of time, allowing space for the person to make different choices. The point is you need to have the conversation. Actively disengaged people can have a massively corrosive effect. If this person works for you, it is not sufficient to just hope the problem will go away.

4

What helps people engage?

As we've already seen, there are different versions of what 'engagement' means – does this mean there are different things that prompt us to get engaged? Of course. This is where a model will help.

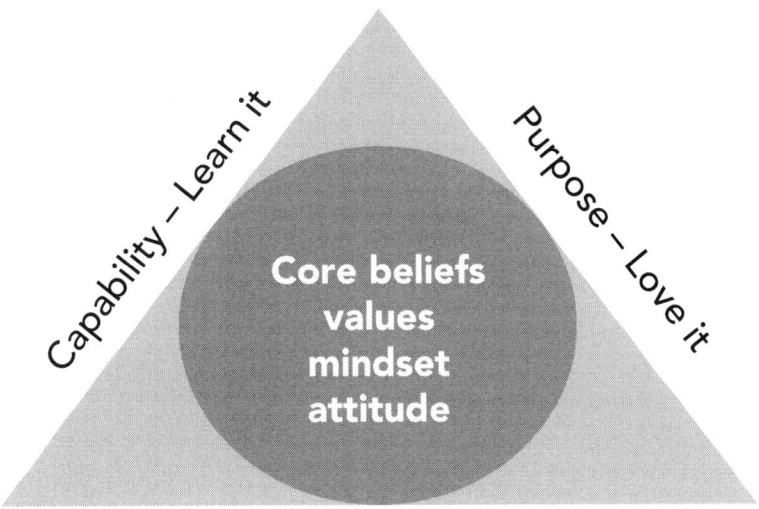

Figure 2: Motivational triangle

There are lots of versions of the motivational triangle[7], and this is mine – a bit of a collage of the others.

Essentially, we feel most motivated when we are doing something that has meaning to us (purpose), we have the skills, knowledge and support to allow us to reach the goal (we are capable) and we have sufficient control over what we do for us to feel part of the solution.

> *Mindset: it's what I believe I can do*
>
> Kenton Cool in 2013 set a world first with his climbing partner Dorje Gylogen when they climbed Nuptse (7,861m), Everest (8,848m) and Lhotse (8,516m) in one trip. It was the 11th time Cool had reached the summit of Everest.
>
> Much earlier in Cool's climbing history, he had fallen and shattered both heels, and still suffers pain. He could have decided at that point that climbing wasn't for him. The fact that he not only resumed climbing but went on to achieve such renown is a testament to his mindset. He is a climber, that's what he does.
>
> Another example come from Mike Newman, who drove a Porsche 911 at 186mph in September 2013 to set a new land speed record. He's blind. But speed is what he does.

How we individually view these three drivers is governed to a great extent by our core values and mindset. These things form the framework in which we make choices about how we respond to the challenges around us. How do we connect these motivational drivers with engagement?

We can pretty easily attach the characteristics that we see in highly engaged people to the motivational triangle.

---

[7] Among the many theories on motivation I would recommend Cranston & Keller's work on the 'meaning quotient' – we need to connect to something intellectually and emotionally, and we need to know it matters; and Daniel Pink's *"Drive"* – there's a good 10 minute YouTube version of this

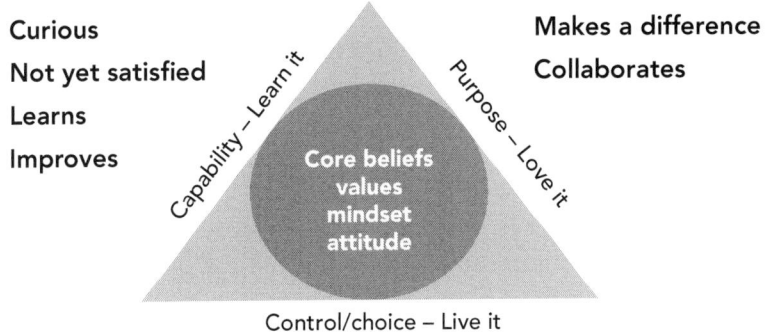

Figure 3: Motivational triangle and characteristics of engagement

Purpose

This links back to our first definition of 'engagement' as a verb: 'participating in something to achieve something'. That last bit is important: 'to achieve something'. We can all think of activities we do – watching a black and white film on a wet, cold Saturday afternoon – where we are certainly engrossed in the activity (particularly in my case if it happens to be a Hitchcock movie), but it doesn't particularly achieve anything (other than to provide me with an entertaining afternoon). That isn't sufficient in a corporate world, or indeed where any individual is working with others to achieve a shared outcome.

If achieving something, or purpose, is important to my engagement, I first of all need to understand what it is and identify why it is important to me.

Simon Sinek tells a great story in his explanation of The Compelling Why[8]. In it he tells the story of two teams of people who were both intent on developing the first aeroplane. One team had all the resources (funding, people, knowledge) that you could ever desire; the other team

---

[8] Simon Sinek on TED talks (www.ted.com/talks): how great leaders inspire action

had the Wright brothers. They had a tiny fraction of the resources of their competitors, but they had a burning conviction and determination to develop a flying machine. We don't even remember the name of their competitors.

Let's put some of that into a more familiar context. You run an operations team, delivering products to customers. You have goals that say you need to do this faster and with greater accuracy. Of course, those are reasonable goals, but when I was that operations manager, they weren't the goals that made me get up in the morning wanting to do a good job. Instead, I needed to translate these into the effect on the customer: what would happen if I delivered something that was of poor quality or that was late in getting to them?

Let's look at something small scale: you run an on-line book shop and have just received an order for a book of poetry, you've got one in stock, but it's been there a while and is a bit grubby…. You're sure it will be fine; the customer might not notice. But the customer does notice and feels really disappointed because the book was a gift for someone to say a special thank you.

Now lets scale it up: your team produces a gadget that helps reduce the incidence of infection for people who need to have catheters while they're in hospital. Poor quality or late supplies mean more people suffer infections, complicating their primary health challenge, and have to have longer stays in hospital, putting a strain on them and their families….

Both outcomes can be avoided if people truly understand the value they bring. In the first scenario, you weren't delivering a book – you were helping someone say thank you; in the second, you weren't delivering a clinical device – you were helping to keep that person free of infection, allowing them to get back to their family as soon as possible. If we think in this way, there is a much greater likelihood of us doing all we can to deliver a great outcome for the customer – we truly engage in our jobs.

Capability

On May 25th 1961 John F Kennedy announced to a special joint session of Congress that the US would put an American on the moon by the end of the decade. This was an audacious goal and the announcement was audaciously timed – on May 5th Russia had safely put a man into space. The space race inspired many people to expand their thinking, and the science it fostered sowed the seeds for many of the technological advancements we now take for granted.

This was a truly awesome goal – but it wouldn't have driven me to a higher level of motivation or engagement. I failed my A level Physics and have adopted a mindset that I'm not a scientist. I wouldn't have had the skills to get involved and without this, all I can be is a bystander.

Mihaly Csikszentmihalyi produced a very helpful way for us to look at our capabilities with the concept of flow[9]. He was essentially looking at how we can achieve happiness, and suggested this would be achieved when our capabilities matched the level of challenge. Although engagement is not the same as happiness, I think Csikszentmihalyi's flow model helps us to understand when capability aids engagement. If we are in flow, our skills match our challenges – we are competent and effective. In this state (as compared with being in a state of anxiety or boredom) we can choose to engage in what we are doing and throw ourselves into the task at hand.

We can easily translate this to our world. Think of your move to line leadership. In many companies, line leaders are promoted from the ranks. By itself, that wouldn't be too bad, but often when we put people into new roles, we don't alter our expectations of what they can achieve: 'they were great in their old role, they'll be great in this one….' Each new role has a learning curve attached, and when the roles are very different (technical to people management), it is harsh and unrealistic to expect immediate competence in the new role. Their skill levels aren't

---

[9] M Csikszentmihalyi, *"Flow: the classic work on how to achieve happiness"*, 2002

sufficient to meet the level of challenge. This is a bit like throwing a non-swimmer into the deep end of the pool to 'see how they get on'. No wonder we're in a state of anxiety.

Moving this dire picture on a bit, we receive some great training and have the help of a good mentor; we learn how to manage and lead people. Now our skills match the expectations made of us – we are in Flow. In this place, I'm competent and I can make a difference to the people I lead. Of course, being in Flow doesn't mean I stop learning. If I'm engaged with what I'm doing, I will be continuing to learn and develop my capabilities – allowing me to get better at what I do as a line leader.

Control

Imagine that I am giving you a lottery ticket for free. I've chosen the numbers for you. They are 5-24-17-81-9.

A bit later, I ask if I can buy it back from you. Make a note of what you will charge me.

Now imagine that I am giving you, another free lottery ticket but this time you get to choose what numbers you would like on your lottery ticket. Make a note of the numbers you choose. Why did you choose those numbers? Why are they important to you? Now when I ask to buy the ticket from you, what price are you going to ask for it?

The likelihood is that you will ask a higher price for the ticket where you chose the number. We are more attached to things we have some perceived control over (hence we put a higher price on them). In reality there is no difference in the probability of either lottery ticket winning the jackpot, so they should be of equal monetary value.[10]

Another way of looking at this is using the Control Continuum, again used by the human performance experts at K2.

---

[10] See the works on behavioral economics and decision-making biases by Daniel Kahneman and Amos Tversky

Imagine a line: one end of the continuum represents a place where you have no control over what you do or how you do it; at the other end you have total control.

Take a moment to recall a situation where you had no control: e.g. you were told what to do and how to do it, every step was prescribed to you, you were not allowed to deviate from the plan and your every step was monitored. Now think about the other end of the scale, where you had total control of what you did and/or how you did it. You might have had a boss who explained the overall goal, but you could then decide how you would get to this goal and put this plan into action.

No Control	Total Control
Describe your experience	Describe your experience
How did you feel about this?	How did you feel about this?
What did you feel about the objective when you set out?	What did you feel about the objective when you set out?

How you felt about these activities will of course depend on what they were and how comfortable you were doing them. When we encounter something for the first time, it can be very daunting if we are not shown how to do it or given some guidance (think about your first day in your first job).

As we become more experienced and capable around a certain activity, it is likely that we become more comfortable with making our own choices about how we tackle it (and frustrated if we don't have this freedom). We may still be doing something that has a distinct outcome (we need to deliver a service to a customer or reach a certain sales target), and if we have the freedom to approach the task in the way that makes the most of our strengths, this is likely to feel more satisfying or fulfilling because we're more involved in the process.

5

What happens when we put these things together?

It is relatively easy to work out what motivates us at an individual level.

Think about a time when you felt really happy about something you were doing or had achieved. What was going on that made you feel happy about the situation?

It is likely that you valued what you were doing; you had a strong sense of purpose. You will also have had the skills you needed to achieve your goal, though you may not have been certain of this when you set out (often we get our greatest sense of achievement when we successfully tackle something we were a bit apprehensive about). It is also likely you will have had a say in how you achieved your goal – you will have made choices and been involved. All of this adds up to you feeling motivated and engaged.

The tale of a 1950 little, grey Fergie called Eleanor

Eleanor came into my life because I was being flippant about what to write in the aspiration box in my corporate-directed leadership development plan: "I want to do a great job so I can buy a tractor."

Roll-on some years, and I have now told various people about this and they start to indulge me…. I get a tractor calendar one year, a tractor mug the next. Then I spot a photo of Eleanor for sale. I dismiss the fact that I have no land, had never driven a tractor and didn't have anywhere to put her, and buy her anyway.

Since then, flippancy has been replaced with something more robust. Eleanor has purpose: she pulls the boat to the jetty, she featured in our son's wedding, she gave me a story to write for our grand-daughter and she is a fabulous conversation piece. I've increased my skills: I can now drive her (don't remind me about missing the turning to the local agricultural show because I was going too fast – 12 miles an hour!) and enjoy keeping her paintwork up to scratch. She is important to me, and I can do something to keep her in good shape – this is an active state of engagement.

Finding our own motivational recipe is one thing but many of the things we do in the business world do not come down to one individual. Many things we seek to achieve can only be gained by working with others.

This is rarely easy, not least because the motivations of everyone involved will be slightly different – each person needs to make a personal connection.

I see it working like this:

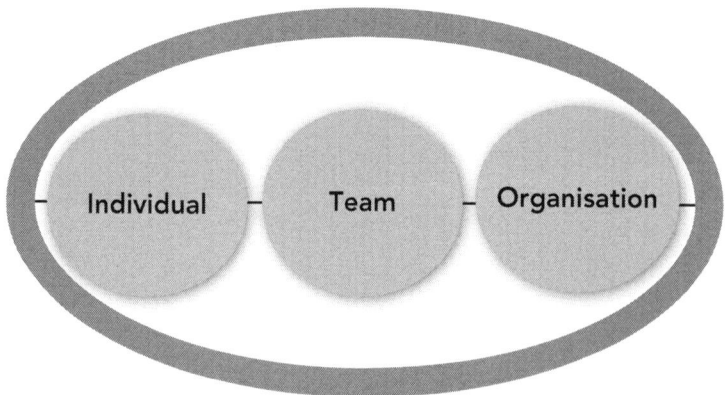

Figure 4: Rugby ball model of engagement

The three rings depict the individual, their team, and the organisation. In this picture, they are shown in perfect alignment. The line running through them depicts the common purpose that joins them together. Each of the three spheres exists within the outer rugby ball, which depicts our environment and culture, and signifies how we go about achieving our goals. These are the processes we use, the way we behave and the values that guide our decisions and choices. Within this culture (the white space), we have the elements of capability and control. We have the right skill sets and degree of control over how we use them.

In this state of perfect alignment, we have created the conditions for optimum engagement. I want to achieve what my team wants to achieve, and my team wants to achieve what my organisation wants to achieve. Moreover, my organisation, team and I achieve this outcome by behaving in a predictable, understood way, in an environment where we make optimum use of relevant skills and exercise appropriate levels of control.

An important point to make here is that while the behaviours are predictable (meaning we don't have to spend a lot of time working out how to behave with each other), and the individual, team and organisation are in alignment, this does not mean it is always harmonious or that people are acquiescent.

For this to work, there has to be room for different opinions and constructive debate. The alignment is that we all know, understand and sign up to a common purpose and general way of working to achieve that purpose. However, the specific strategies and tactics we might use to reach our goal will be much stronger if they are reached through debate and consensus forming. This allows the team to consider new approaches to a problem and remain agile.

It also lowers the dangers of group-think, where members of the group coalesce around an idea simply because that person is a designated leader, a master influencer or knows how to shout the loudest. It is possible that the group in this case comes up with a bright idea that achieves a great outcome. However, the group-think short-cut means we skipped the bit where we thoroughly scrutinised the idea, tested it, improved it or decided to ditch bits of it because it doesn't stack up. All of which would have led to an even better idea and outcome, and a greater sense of ownership.

These opinions don't just spring from my own observations of how teams work. They are also frequently cited in the plethora of research on teams and what makes them effective (or defective). One of the classic team models that has a lot of practical credence is Patrick Lencioni's "The Five Dysfunctions of a Team".[11]

This model argues that teams fail (or are dysfunctional) because there is absence of trust, fear of conflict, lack of commitment, avoidance of accountability and inattention to results. Turn these to the positive – a team who trust each other, seek and know how to handle constructive conflict, are committed to what they do, make themselves accountable and focus on results – and it is easy to see the parallels to the rugby-ball model of engagement.

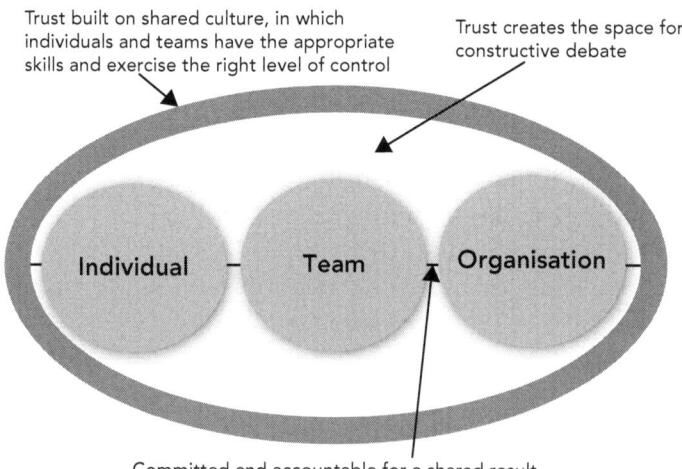

Figure 5: Rugby-ball model and the team dynamic

---

[11] Further reading: Patrick Lencioni "The five dysfunctions of a team: a leadership fable", 2002 and "Overcoming the five dysfunctions of a team", 2005

The line through the middle is all about commitment, accountability and focus on a shared goal — it is what binds the actions of individuals and teams. The rugby ball meanwhile encapsulates the foundations of trust.

Trust is built around shared purpose and flourishes when two parties know what they're doing together, why they're doing it and how they're going to go about it. We also put our trust in others far more easily when we have mutual respect and believe they have the necessary skills to carry out their task. If we don't believe they can and will do what they say they will do, we are unlikely to cede control to them.

When we trust people, we also have an environment that doesn't just cope with differences of opinion and conflict, but actively generates debate and acknowledges there are different ways of doing something. We can do this because we know that the person arguing with us is doing so because they think they have a better way of achieving our common goal; they are not arguing with us because they want to look better than us, or are pursuing an agenda that is different to ours.

So we have a model developed from working with people, teams and organisations, and backed up by a far more thoroughly researched model around teams. However, like Lencioni, I always think it is useful to test any model from the reverse side. What does it look like when things are not working in the optimum way? Consider what it means if a person or team are not in an aligned state, but are off doing their own thing.

We can test this with a story and a character called Joe. In both versions of the model (the aligned and non-aligned), Joe comes into work and gets on with something.

In the aligned version, Joe shares the same goals as his team and his company and they feel important to him.

Joe's company makes high-spec widgets that are used in the aircraft industry and Joe, a skilled technician, is proud to tell people he helps to keep people in the air.

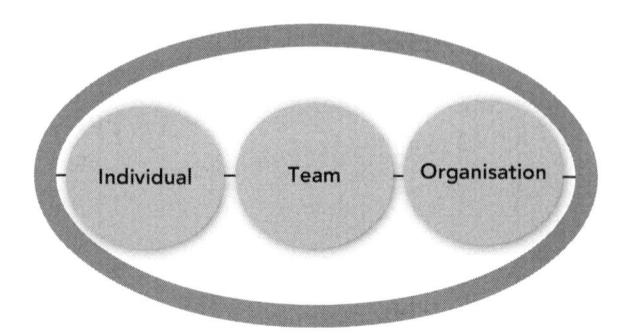

```
  Individual  —  Team  —  Organisation
```
(Individual, Team, and Organisation shown as three overlapping circles within a single enclosing ellipse)

He understands how he, his team and the company will work together to achieve the goals. In Joe's case he is responsible for setting up and maintaining two precision boring machines – if they are not set up correctly, the final widgets won't fit properly, potentially causing catastrophic damage to an aeroplane's wings.

He has the right skill set and attitude, and consistently makes good choices about how he will apply these: Joe makes sure he knows everything there is to know about the current machines and is part of the team designing the next, more efficient version.

In this aligned state, because everyone is pulling in the same direction, focused on achieving the same thing, and behaving in the same way, there is a much higher likelihood that Joe, his team and the company will be successful in their aims.

In the unaligned, or misaligned, version Joe doesn't really understand what the company's goals are or how he contributes to them, and they certainly don't feel important to him:

Joe's aim each day is to see how fast he can get through his assigned quota of widgets, so he makes sure the machines are working efficiently, but he's not always careful about the quality of what's being produced – that doesn't feature in how he's paid and surely it won't matter if a few widgets are a bit substandard?

WHAT HAPPENS WHEN WE PUT THESE THINGS TOGETHER? | 33

He also doesn't understand what the company is talking about when they go on about 'values' and 'our culture' - it is a happy coincidence if his behaviours match up to the ones the company is trying to cultivate; he often behaves counter-culturally – quality isn't at the top of his mind.

However, Joe is quite a sociable bloke and he likes the people who work around him – they feel like family. Joe would help them out if they needed it and it didn't put him to too much trouble.

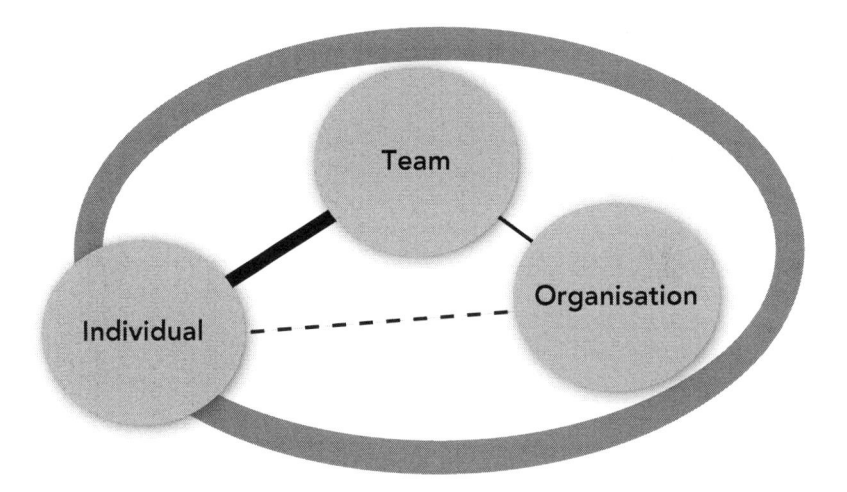

Figure 6: Unaligned model of engagement

In this version, at best, it is a coincidence if Joe's efforts benefit the company; at worst, his actions could be extremely detrimental (when a plane falls out of the sky because its wings have fallen off).

6

What can I do about engagement?

There is a difficulty with both engagement and motivation. You can't do either of them to someone. You cannot make me engage in something; nor can you make me feel motivated. Both are individual choices: I choose to engage, and I choose to feel motivated (or not).

If this is true, should we stop this book right here? If it is up to an individual whether they choose to engage or not, what has engagement got to do with managers and leaders in a business? Even if we can do something about it, isn't this a job for HR?

I have great respect for my HR colleagues. Over the years, they have given pertinent guidance and support as I learnt how to manage people. They have kept me legal and helped me find the right line between leading with compassion and managing people to get a job done. They have also contributed greatly to the mission of creating an engaged workforce – it cannot happen without them.

But – and this is a big **BUT** – it is the team, department and functional managers and leaders that have the greatest influence on their teams and the greatest opportunity to create (or destroy) an environment in which full engagement is the norm, not a 'nice to have'. And this is nothing to do with liking people or being altruistic. As a leader of people, in an operational setting, with a list of goals and targets to achieve, it is in my interest to create an environment where I get the most from the people who work with me. Otherwise I am tying one hand behind my back before I even start – not a comfortable thing to do!

The key premise then is that it is **our job as leaders and managers in a business to create an engaging environment where people choose to engage.** How do we do this? The motivational drivers give us three primary levers to work with:

1. **Purpose:** knowing why you are doing what you are doing
2. **Capability:** making sure people have the relevant skills and information to allow them to contribute
3. **Control:** giving people the freedom and framework to choose how they achieve their goals.

We need to be working on all three. It is not sufficient to have people who are highly skilled, but who don't understand how to apply their capabilities or what they are seeking to do. Equally, we will not get very far with people who are fired up by the mission they are on, but who lack the skills needed to truly participate. I'm pretty sure the idea of putting a man on the moon would still be a dream if was not for the highly skilled engineers who worked out how to turn this into a reality.

But where to start? Is this a chicken-and-egg scenario – which comes first: capability, control or purpose? Of course we are not starting with a blank sheet of paper. Most organisations are already up and running and will have some sort of purpose, individuals in that organisation will have a certain set of skills, and will be exercising them according to the prevailing management systems. That said, I think we can look at these levers in order and apply a process that will transform our environments into places where full engagement is the norm rather than a haphazard happy coincidence. This process is called Connecting People[12]:

---

[12] Julie Goodwin, co-founder of Vybrant, an innovative leadership development company whose mission is to 'make people more valuable' gave me invaluable help in joining the dots of my research and devising the Connecting People process http://www.vybrant.org

WHAT CAN I DO ABOUT ENGAGEMENT? | 37

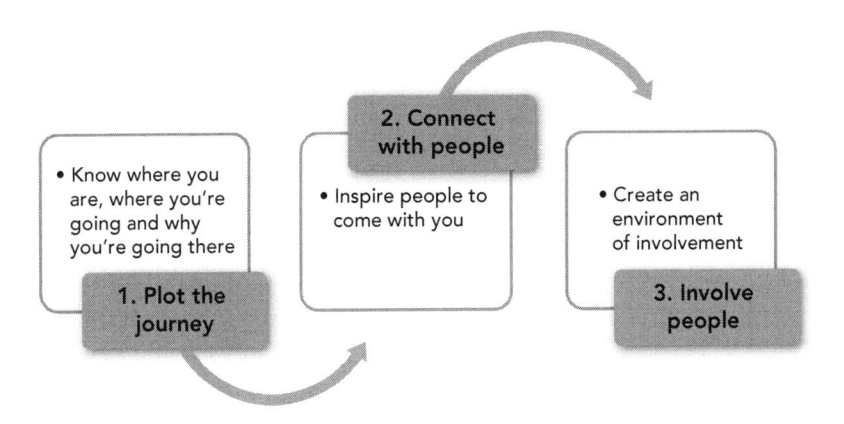

1. Plot the journey
- Know where you are, where you're going and why you're going there

2. Connect with people
- Inspire people to come with you

3. Involve people
- Create an environment of involvement

Figure 7: Connecting people

At its most basic, the first two steps are about creating and sharing **Purpose**. Without this, we might have all the skill and will in the world, but only be applying it randomly.

The third step is all about developing people and creating an environment in which they can apply their capabilities (**Capability** and **Control**).

The next few chapters delve into each of these stages in turn, putting more detail behind them. Each breaks down into three parts:

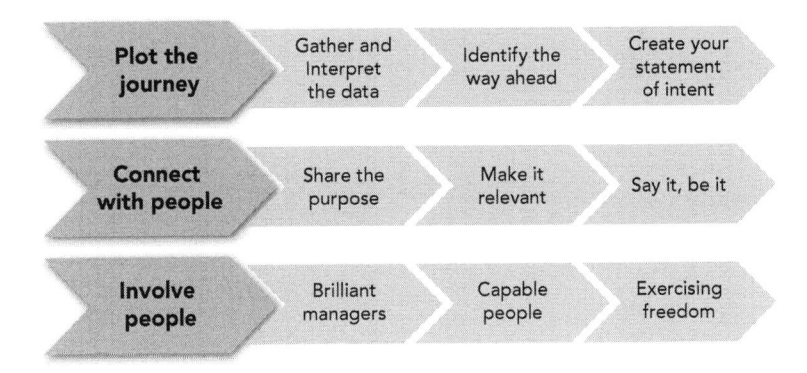

Plot the journey	Gather and Interpret the data	Identify the way ahead	Create your statement of intent
Connect with people	Share the purpose	Make it relevant	Say it, be it
Involve people	Brilliant managers	Capable people	Exercising freedom

Figure 8: Connecting people in a bit more detail

7

Plot the journey

Plot the journey › Gather and Interpret the data › Identify the way ahead › Create your statement of intent

Plotting the journey is about knowing where you are and working out where you want to go.

Why is this important?

This is the bit that gives you and your organisation **purpose** – one of our motivational drivers. In a very practical sense it is also the bit that will help to frame the decisions and choices you make as an organisation:

Shire

The pioneering pharmaceutical company Shire is all about purpose. The company exists to be 'brave'. This one word represents their business model, the people they help and their staff: they develop niche medical interventions that help people with life-changing, often rare, illnesses, and make brave decisions that push the boundaries of what was previously considered possible. Brave might also be applied to their growth plans. After a failed takeover by AbbVie in 2014, Shire's purchase of NPS in 2015 reaffirms its independence and bravery: while NPS clearly fits the Shire profile (it has two rare disease products), it didn't make a profit during 30-years in business.

If you are in a senior role within an organisation, it is your job to be setting its direction. But, all leaders and managers within an organisation also need to be able to do this with their teams.

This can be particularly hard for middle managers, who need to be able to translate the overall direction of the company, and the decisions made by those with greater authority, into the work their team is engaged in. And not just in the form of a list of actions. Middle managers, like senior leaders, need to be able to translate why they are doing what they are doing, as well as explaining how they are going to do it. There is more on this art form in the next section on *Connect with people*.

For now, let's concentrate on plotting the journey.

Unless you are a start up, you will already be on a journey. Your organisation already exists to do something, and has already worked out how it's going to do it (more or less). If this purpose is still 'fit for purpose', great – skip to the next section. However, journeys have a habit of changing and the velocity of that change is increasing:

D&B

Dun & Bradstreet set out on 20th July 1841 to provide information on businesses with a view to helping them trade on the right terms. This remains their core purpose, but the manner in which they do this has changed dramatically. Some of the changes have been imposed on the company (it is difficult to keep pace in the digital age and explosion of data) but D&B has also frequently been at the forefront of technological advances: putting in one of the first mass orders for typewriters to equip its reporters, through to developing a unique classification system to allow a single view of a customer to be established (a requirement that sits at the centre of much of the new regulation surrounding banks).

Technology advancements have changed both how D&B goes about its business and the scope of its business. Both of these dynamics need to be understood and explained to customers and employees alike.

I can't think of an organisation where change doesn't happen in some shape or form. Added to this, the very process of change is dynamic: we rarely go straight from A to B.

"The best laid schemes o' mice an' men gang aft agley"[13]

It is this dynamic quality that makes the task of plotting the journey particularly difficult. If nothing changed, you could work out your purpose, plot the journey and share it with your staff just once. Job done.

If this seems an unlikely scenario, we need to consider how we go about identifying our purpose in a changing world.

Gather the data

We start by working out where we are currently. There are lots of tools to help us with this:

- *Talking with and listening to people* – there is no substitute for regular, face-to-face conversations with the people. Ask, listen, observe (does what people say match how they behave? If not, why not).

- Your organisation's *performance metrics* and *customer case studies* will give you a picture of how things are currently as

---

[13] A far less poetic rendition: 'our best laid plans often go wrong', Robert Burns *"To a Mouse"*, 1785

long as they go beyond the purely financial outputs and also look at things such as quality, speed of service and employee well-being.

- *SWOT analysis* helps us to understand our organisation's strengths and weaknesses, as well as the external opportunities and threats[14].

- The *PESTEL*[15] (political, economic, social, technology, environmental, legal) and *Porter's 5 Forces*[16] tools are helpful in understanding our external environment at a macro and micro level.

- The *Cultural Web*[17], or tools of that kind, help to shed light on what sort of culture we operate in in our organisations. For those readers who just flinched at the word 'culture', you need to be mindful of its power. Culture exists whether we like it or not. It captures how we do things and influences our agility and how we make decisions and choices. It is fundamental to how every organisation operates.

- Of course, this being a book about engagement, there are also lots of survey and audit tools that help measure the levels of engagement at any particular point in time.

---

[14] There are different opinions on who invented the SWOT framework, but most sources seem to credit Albert Humphrey, working at the Stanford Research Institute, as its originator.

[15] The origins of the PESTEL tool (originally PEST) are unclear – it is widely used across businesses and has been through many iterations.

[16] E.g. see ME Porter *"The five competitive forces that shape strategy"*, Harvard Business Review, Jan 2008

[17] E.g. see G Johnson, R Whittington, K Scholes *"Fundamentals of Strategy"*, Pearson Education, 2012

Surveys – uses and abuses

Surveys are useful tools – I've even developed one with K2[18]. But they come with a number of pitfalls.

Of my three main concerns, the first two – the parent-child contract, and the paint-the-walls-a-different-colour syndrome – centre around transactional engagement ("I'll do this for you, if you'll do that for me"); the third – engagement in isolation – centres on the missed opportunity to think about engagement in a transformational way.

Parent-child contract

Many surveys ask a standard set of questions based on a pre-described model of engagement. This is what helps them achieve consistency, and allows a company to benchmark itself against others.

However, this 'one-size-fits-all' approach typically starts at the wrong point and often focuses on a fairly rudimentary set of drivers. For instance, in one particular survey, the questions centred on:

- Work – tasks, processes, resources, sense of accomplishment
- People – senior leadership, leader, colleagues, people focus, customers
- Opportunities – learning and development, career opportunities
- Total rewards – pay, benefits, recognition
- Company practices – HR, managing performance, brand alignment, organisation reputation, diversity, change
- Quality of life – physical work environment, work/life balance

---

[18] The High Performance Culture Audit (http://www.planetk2.com). This tool looks at how a team is performing, with engagement being seen as a product of high performance.

These drivers are unsurprising and have some merit: we like to feel we are paid fairly and recognised for our work; we like to feel confident about our leaders and enjoy the company of our colleagues; we like to work in a nice place, and have sufficient flexibility to feel our work and home lives can both be accommodated. You could put many of these factors into the model of motivation explored in the chapter on *What helps people engage?*

But all these things, and the way they are presented, are also very parent-child in nature. They implicitly say: "I will give you these things as your employer, and in return expect you to be fully committed to your work".

I'm not going to turn down a pay rise or private health cover, but this doesn't really fit well with the picture of a highly engaged person (see *How do engaged and disengaged people behave?*).

In particular, this approach doesn't seem to take account of the fact that highly engaged people don't wait for someone else to engage them but take responsibility for their own engagement, or that you can find highly engaged people in a wide variety of settings – some with great office spaces and lucrative salaries, but many working in environments that don't have these things. These sorts of questions also tell me very little about the mindset of the individuals and whether they are visibly demonstrating their engagement.

Surveys are also susceptible to the problem we're probably all guilty of where we say one thing yet behave otherwise. This is the bit where parent-child behaviours trip up the child. For instance, the survey might ask (paraphrasing from a number of different surveys): *"Are you clear on the strategy set out by your senior leaders"*. To which we typically say *"No"*.

This might be absolutely true – we're not clear. But this response shields the fact that I've chosen not to attend the last three strategy presentations and never read the weekly newsletter or watch the CEO's monthly video on the state of the business. Again, very parent-child: I've ceded responsibility for my understanding of the company's strategy to the senior leaders; it is up to them to make sure I'm clear on it and their fault if I'm not.

These surveys have some value – they tell you what a large number of people think about the issues you've asked about.

The two key bits of advice would be to make sure you are asking about the right things (the things that will help people participate to the best of their ability in your organisation), and are positioning the survey as a measurement tool, not a component of the parent-child contract.

What information could you use to gauge your team's level of participation:

Gauging participation	
What sort of participation are you looking to encourage?	
What metrics could you use to give you a measure of engagement?	

What questions could you ask your team? What would they tell you?	
What would you do with this information?	

Paint-the-walls-a-different colour syndrome

By perpetuating a parent-child environment that asks "What don't you like?"[19] and then seeks to fix it, we can potentially fall into one of two traps.

The first is that the action plans and initiatives this approach encourages are perceived as ways for the organisation to simply get more out of its workers. Think I'm being cynical? Consider this:

The survey asks about work-life balance.

- The results show this is a problem that is getting in the way of people engaging more fully.

---

[19] Note – this is also an easy trap to fall into - thinking of engagement in terms of whether our employees are happy with something. Engagement ≠ Happiness

- The organisation invests money in an on-site crèche that is open for our children from 7 in the morning to 7 at night.
- Do I see this as being helpful (I might have two young children to look after, and this has just made my life much easier)? Or is this just the company making it easier for me to work longer hours for their own benefit (I no longer feel I can leave at 5pm to pick my kids up)?

Sometimes even the best of intentioned ideas will be seen like this. If an organisation goes down this route be open about it: "we (all the parents with kids and the organisation) both win from this".

The second trap is more invidious and involves us 'doing engagement activities' because we want to be seen to be doing something, or even worse, because the leaders in the business have a set of bonus goals that only pay out if they raise the engagement score from x to y. This leads into one of the most dangerous areas of survey abuse – the 'paint-the-walls-a-different-colour' syndrome.

This scenario runs something like this:

- We do a survey and analyse the results.
- We see that people don't like their physical working environment.
- We assume this is because the walls are painted a ghastly green.
- We repaint the walls yellow and everyone smiles.
- At the next survey, people still don't like their working environment.
- We scratch our heads - it can't be the walls, we've just painted them.
- This time we ask some people around the business what it is they like and dislike about their working environment, and we

find that there aren't enough hot desks on Mondays when all the team leaders hold their weekly meetings…. It has nothing to do with the colour of the walls, and everything to do with removing an obstacle that has prevented people from working efficiently.

This scenario is very real, and I've certainly fallen into this trap on more than one occasion.

The one that sticks most painfully in my mind was when a survey response showed people were dissatisfied with the career development at this particular organisation. Having recently been to a lecture on the subject, I leapt to the conclusion that this was because there were no clear job families and progression paths, and launched a project with my HR business partner to put these in place.

Of course, this was good practice. However, it wasn't the key issue for the people taking the survey. When I finally got round to asking people what they thought would improve career development in the organisation, they said: "It would really help if HR sent an email out each month telling us what jobs are being advertised…" - somewhat easier to achieve than the project I had just launched.

The key thing to note is that interpreting surveys from a spreadsheet is dangerous – consult widely to get to the nub of the issue, and then provide a framework to help people resolve the issue themselves (see *Involve people*).

Engagement in isolation

Often surveys appear to treat 'engagement' as something that sits in glorious isolation, detached from the ambitions, context and culture of the organisation for which we work. This is possibly why 'engagement' gets dismissed as being 'soft and fluffy', and a 'nice to have', rather than a crucial element of strategic advantage.

If you are not yet convinced of this, re-read the chapter on *Why bother?* Then do a comparison of two parts of your organisation: one that seems dynamic, regularly exceeds its ambitions and has people hammering on the door to join; and one that struggles to reach its target each year and is haemorrhaging people. Which do you think has the higher level of engagement among its people?

Now extend this to the outside world. First, imagine yourself as a consumer. You are off to buy the latest TV. You've done your research and found two models you think you like and two retailers who have both on offer at the same price. You speak with a sales person from each retailer. Who are you going to buy from:

- A: the person who can answer your questions, asks about what you use a TV for and highlights some additional features you would find useful and makes sure it can be delivered in the most convenient way to you; or

- B: the person who assumes you mainly use a TV for playing games and watching sport, disappears off for 20 minutes to get some more information on insurance, and then tells you they can deliver in a week between 8am and 10pm that day?

You may think this is about training (product knowledge) and processes (delivery times), but in the first case, the person is showing an appropriate interest in you, they are curious enough to find out what you use the product for, they are knowledgeable about what they are selling, they appreciate you might not want to be hanging around waiting for a delivery; we could connect many of these attributes with the characteristics of engagement (see *How do engaged and disengaged people behave?*).

In the second case, there is none of this curiosity – the person's been given training and a script and a process and is sticking to it – and no indication that they remotely care which TV is the right one for you or whether the delivery arrangements are convenient.

Now, consider the same scenario in terms of someone buying from your organisation and a competitor. Who is a customer more likely to buy from?

Some of the decision will be down to product and price, but the experience that customer has of the people in your organisation will also play a part (bearing in mind this includes people directly selling or servicing a customer and those who send the invoices, process payments, invent and improve the products, hire and develop great people…). If people make a difference to the customer-buying decision, they are of strategic importance to your business, and their level of engagement is a key part of your unique competitive edge (see *Building profitable, long-lasting customer relationships*).

The word 'unique' has not been used by accident. We've established that highly engaged people share some characteristics; how they apply them is unique to each individual.

If we look back at a couple of examples used earlier in the book (see *What is engagement?*), for Katherine Grainger it appears that tenacity is a key part of her engagement framework: no-one wins that many elite-class medals without this. What came across in the case of the spare-parts mechanic helping to fix our daughter's car was the ability to appreciate our worries and apply his expert knowledge in a way that was truly helpful.

It is the same with teams (which are collections of individuals) and organisations (which are collections of teams). For me as an individual, it is not sufficient to be 'enthusiastic'; to be highly engaged is to participate to the full extent of my abilities to achieve something I value. For a team or organisation, it is about everyone who works in it collectively participating to the full extent of our abilities to achieve something we collectively value. The thing that we value will determine how we need to engage or participate.

To illustrate what I mean, let me introduce you to the fictitious company, Lowestever Air. Three key things stand out as important to the company. If the company doesn't pay attention to these things, it will not survive:

1. **Safety:** Everyone at Lowestever Air has to be focused on safety – whether this is aircraft maintenance, luggage handling, or making sure people have not packed dangerous items in their bags. Without this focus, passengers (and others) are at risk. They will quickly be out of business if planes start falling out of the sky.

2. **Teamwork:** It is critical that people at Lowestever Air work as a team, whether they are front desk, luggage handlers, aircraft maintenance or aircrew. They need to work together to minimise the aircraft's time on the ground and give customers a great experience so that they travel with Lowestever Air again.

3. **Reliability:** It is vital that the aircraft are where they need to be, and that the staff is available to check-in, service and dispatch aircraft efficiently and on time.

For this company, the 'engagement recipe' (how people participate in Lowestever Air) may focus heavily on **collaboration** in an environment where individuals take **ownership** of situations, and are **accountable** for providing a safe, reliable service to customers.

In our second fictitious company, Mostamazing Apps, what's important is the ability of its staff to be continually inventing the next 'can't live without that app'. To do this it is probably essential that the people working there are **curious, innovative** and **seek to push back today's boundaries**.

In both cases, having highly engaged people, participating in particular ways to the full extent of their abilities, are going to give those companies sharp competitive edges that make them more likely to succeed. Engagement, and the engagement recipe, is of strategic importance, not an optional extra or something to survey just because you happen to be in the habit of measuring every aspect of your business that you can.

To survey or not to survey?

Given these dire warnings, you might think that I don't like surveys. You would be wrong. They are useful tools.

Surveys give us a snapshot of the level of engagement at a given time, in a consistent way, across a group of people. We can compare sub-sets, look at the whole, review alongside previous surveys, and spot trends. We can benchmark the results against other groups in our company, industry, country or region. As an analyst, I delight in dicing data, looking at averages, modes, medians and spreads: the data tells me a story.

Moreover, because surveys ask a self-contained set of questions, they lend themselves to action planning and decision-making, which can be a useful starting point when working with teams who are not yet engaging as a matter of course. But beware: surveys are potent. People like to be asked their opinions but if you then do nothing with them, it can be highly discouraging.

To avoid some of the traps that can occur when 'engagement' is treated as a nice-to-have, transactional process, I would recommend a tailored survey rather than a generic one. This approach has two benefits: engagement 'activities' will be strongly linked to the strategic engagement recipe of the business; and people will have a clear understanding of what is expected of them and what they are helping to achieve (strengthening the sense of purpose and avoiding the parent-child dialogue).

Consider the following:

Survey experience	
Where/when have surveys worked well for you?	
What traps have you fallen into?	
What could you have done differently?	
How are you going to approach the next survey?	

Interpret the data

Once we've gathered our data, the next step is to analyse it to decide whether we are achieving what we want to achieve. If we are not, we need to make changes.

Interpreting data is an art form and comes with a bunch of warnings, summed up by the adage: 'lies, damned lies, and statistics'. I'm a political economist by training, and know there is some truth in this saying. It is not so much that numbers lie – they are sometimes inaccurate but they are also inanimate, incapable of having an intent of their own – rather it is the interpretation of those numbers that can 'lie'.

If we assume malicious intent, then numbers can be used to fabricate all sorts of stories. However, let's assume we are being conscientious, have reasonable analytical skills and want to use the numbers to gain an accurate picture of where we are currently.

We still need to be careful of our own bias – it is very uncomfortable to be faced with a set of numbers that appear to tell you something you don't want to hear or see. Our biases and value base can influence from the very start of the process (in our choice of what information we gather) all the way through to the point where we make decisions. Being more conscious of these biases, and getting a wide enough group of people involved who have different view points, will help to guard against these problems.

The other piece of advice would be to look at trends in both the thing you are looking to measure (engagement, high performance, absenteeism etc.) and wider environmental data. For instance, is there an upturn in absenteeism at the same time as an upturn or downturn in sales, or does absenteeism coincide with unemployment data from the wider economy?

Of course, it is possible to find related trends in all sorts of things that actually have nothing to do with each other (false positives), so always sense check what the statistics seem to be saying. The best way of doing this in my opinion is through regular conversations with others, though again you need to be on your guard for bias. If you only ever ask a particular question of a particular group of people, don't be surprised when you keep getting the same answer back. Mix the questions and the people up and keep your ears and mind open to views that differ from your own.

Identify the way ahead

After gathering and interpreting the data we can conclude one of three things:

1. **Clear skies:** Everything is marvellous: we are achieving the results we want, people are engaged and motivated, our customers are happy and getting the value they need, the path ahead is clear and unchanging.

2. **Distant rumbles of thunder:** Things are okay but could be better: our results are ticking along but are a bit inconsistent, people are generally engaged but absenteeism and turnover are both higher than we would like (we're losing some people we don't want to lose), our customers are starting to shop around and seem to be more price sensitive. We can't see very far ahead – our competitive landscape seems to be changing.

3. **Hurricane season:** Things are going down hill fast: our results are dire, we are haemorrhaging talent and customers. We fear the future and spend our time recounting the past. Our competitors are marching ahead and leaving us behind.

Congratulations if you live in the 'clear skies' scenario: you are already getting it all right and any adjustments you make are likely to be small and taken as a matter of course. Just keep an eye out for changes on the far horizon. For most of us we live in scenario 2 or 3, or somewhere in between. If our analysis tells us things are not as good as they could be (or indeed are dire), we need to make changes, starting with determining what our new destination looks like.

Some of the tools listed above (see *Gather the data*) help us to project forward: what do we think the PESTEL analysis or Porter's 5 Forces will look like in 10, 20, 50 years time? We will also be influenced by our past experiences and by our interpretation of the experience of others (what are other leaders in the industry doing?). I also recommend using the

MAP tool[20]. It can be used in many ways, at an organisation, team or individual level and across different time scales.

Have a go at this exercise to see whether this tool is useful to you. Think of an important event that is coming up in the next couple of months. Use the MAP template and the steps outlined below to think about what you want to achieve and how you're going to go about it. Bear in mind you might want to consider what you're going to stop doing as well.

Goal/event:		
	What are you going to do?	How are you going to do it?
Must		
Aspire		
Phenomenal		

Figure 9: MAP tool

How to use the MAP tool:

- Consider what you must do to achieve a successful outcome (make these actions SMART – specific, measureable, achievable, relevant, time-bound), and how you're going to

---

[20] The MAP tool I've developed has its origins in the Planet K2's MILE tool, which looks at what you Must do, Intend to do, Like to do and what would be Extra or Exceptional; MAP stands for Must, Aspire, Phenomenal

do it (e.g. what strengths are you going to use to achieve these things). Check: you cannot achieve your goal or consider the event a success without these things.

- Consider what you aspire to do, and how you're going to achieve it. Check: you would feel proud if you achieved this.

- Consider what would be truly phenomenal if you achieved it, and how you're going to do it.

- Finally, review your must – you might find it looks or feels too conservative. If it does, go for something more ambitious!

If this helped you focus on the things you need or want to achieve and how you're going to achieve it, your team might also find it useful.

If you want to apply this to a bigger topic, like setting the direction for your business, gather your data and then use the MAP tool to work through these questions, first by yourself and then with your team:

1. What business are you in currently?
2. What business will you be in in 10 years time?
3. What will you be doing in 3 or 5 years time?

One of the things the MAP tool does is to help us come up with goals that are ambitious and inspiring, but we also need to stop and check a few things:

- Is this a highly desirable future state?
    - ☐ What does it allow us to achieve that we don't have today?
    - ☐ Is this really important to us?
    - ☐ What happens if we don't achieve it, how would we feel?
- What competitive advantage will this goal or purpose give you? If the answer is none, don't do it.

- Are you boiling the ocean or warming a puddle?
    - ☐ Does this feel challenging or completely out of reach?
    - ☐ Does it feel familiar enough that you can achieve it but is also sufficiently unfamiliar that it will take you to a different place?
- Why does achieving this matter to you, personally? Are you convinced this is the right thing to aim for? If you can't work this out, you are unlikely to be compelling, authentic or credible when you try to explain it to others.

When you consider the degree of challenge in your goal bear in mind these examples. The first is US President JF Kennedy's ambition to put a man on the moon. This seemed truly out of reach when Kennedy, in May 1961, announced that the US would put a man on the moon by the end of that decade. Not only was this achieved, but we are now planning to put people on Mars: over 200,000 people volunteered for the first one-way mission.

At a less stellar level, consider Roger Bannister's achievement. He was the first person to run a mile in under 4 minutes and he did so despite received medical opinion that our skeletons couldn't cope with stresses like that. He broke through this physical and mental barrier on the 6th of May 1954; he showed the world, and his rivals, that the impossible was possible – his record lasted just 46 days.

Create your statement of intent

You've looked at the data and decided you need to make some changes. You've worked out where you want to get to and it feels desirable and important both to you and the organisation. Now we need to begin the process of working out how we're going to get there.

At this point we are talking about a high-level plan: a statement of intent. It sets out why you are embarking on this journey and where you want to get to in sufficient detail to be credible and convincing. If possible, it will also answer the question that many will ask: "what does it mean for me".

You may need to create a more detailed business case to allow decisions to be made by the senior team, but you should avoid being too detailed at this stage – indeed, doing this would close off a significant opportunity to get people involved (see *Involve people*).

You already have the goal for the statement of intent and the accompanying factors of success. The next step is to identify the activities you're going to undertake to get you to your destination. As you collect the list of possibilities, there are 3 key things to think about:

1. **Use your strengths:** Are there existing competencies that you identified as part of your SWOT analysis that you could use to help push the change through? Also, are there any initiatives already underway that you could accelerate to help you achieve change faster?

2. **Remove barriers:** What are the things you do as a team or organisation that support your current goals but will get in the way as you look to make changes? These need to be removed if you are going to move forward.

3. **Address the gap:** What competencies will you need in this future state, and where are the gaps with your current range of abilities?

Let us go back to our fictitious airline, Lowestever Air (see *Surveys – uses and abuses*). They want to be the cheapest, safest airline in the UK. They know that safety, teamwork and reliability are very important to their success. They are very good at safety, pretty good at reliability, but suffer from poor teamwork, mainly because there is a lack of mutual respect between teams in different parts of the organisation.

Lowestever Air's managers encourage people to share their strong ethos and understanding about safety (**using a strength**) to boost respect for each other and develop a sense of teamwork (**addressing a gap**). This becomes the theme in the reward and recognition scheme, and team profiles and inter-team projects feature regularly in the staff newsletter. They also realise that some of the distrust stems from inconsistent policies on holidays: they get employees together from across the company to work out what a fair holiday policy would be (**removing a barrier**).

Help

High Control

Low impact   Low Control   **High impact**
Low Control

High Control

Hinder

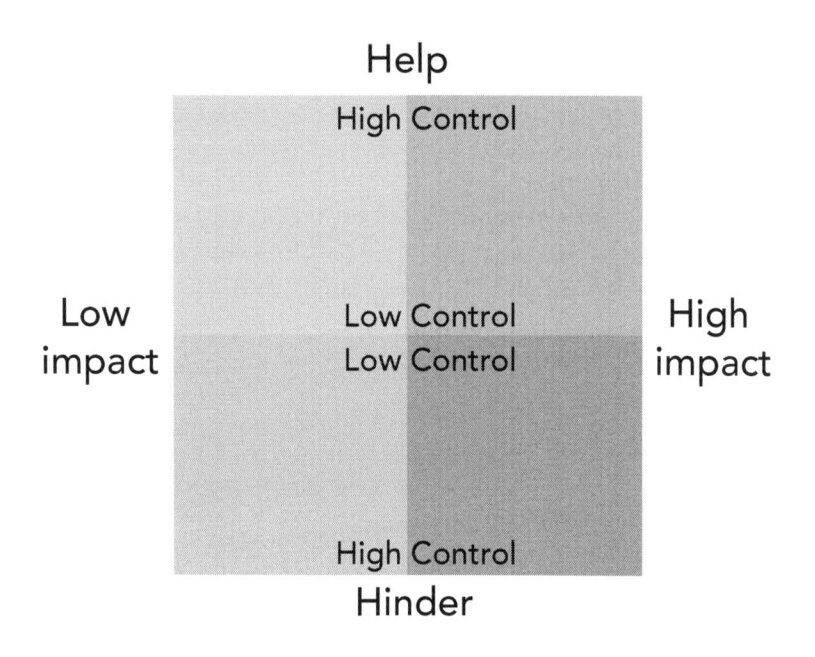

Figure 10: HIC tool

When you start considering all the things you could do, or stop doing, you may end up with a huge list of things. The HIC tool can help you make some choices (see *Appendix: HIC tool – Help, Impact, Control*)[21]. To use this tool, you first decide how much something will help or

---

[21] The Help-Hinder bit of this tool derives from Kurt Lewin's Force Field Analysis, identifying factors that support or oppose a change initiative, while the Control bit has its roots in the control continuum used by K2

hinder you in achieving your goal (**Help/Hinder**); then consider the size of the impact (**Impact**); and finally, how much control you have to change things (**Control**).

Having categorised your actions/behaviours in this way, it is easier to prioritise what you're going to do. Ideally, you would make sure you were using things in the top right corner: they are massively helpful to your cause and you have high control over them. You would also do something about the things getting in your way (in the bottom left square). If you have control over them, that's relatively easy; if you don't have control over them, it is a case of either influencing others or finding a way to limit their impact.

Once you've identified what you could do and whittled this down to what you will do, you can group these actions into related themes. This helps to keep focus and make the tasks more manageable.

A final step is to do the following checks:

- Have you made a strong case for change?
- Do the bits of your plan all link up to achieve your purpose?
- Does the plan answer the question: what does this mean for me (or at least say when this question will be answered)?
- Does the plan show people how they can participate?
- How much time, energy and money will this take (and what's the cost of doing nothing)?
- How will you know when you've been successful or if things aren't going to plan? You don't want to spend all your time measuring progress but you do want to know things are on track.
- When you come up against operational or financial choices, does your purpose and plan help you to decide? For instance, you might have decided that your organisation exists to bring

long-term benefit to your customers. It's quarter end and one of your sales team has the opportunity to sell a product to a customer, helping you reach your target for the year; a product that would better suit the customer's needs will be available next month… Does your purpose help you decide?

It is worth spending time getting the statement of intent right, as it will serve as a strong point of reference as you then embark on the process of bringing the plan to life.

8 | Connect with people

Connect with people → Share the purpose → Make it relevant → Say it, be it

> "Being able to bring the best out in everyone is what ensures a company's success.... It is about how much they are in there with you. A company doesn't run if its people don't run with it." [22]

Share the purpose

You have a goal and a high-level plan. Now you need to share it with other people. That sounds simple, but many organisations seem to miss this step and then wonder why the plan hasn't had the impact expected.

Lots of organisations think they've taken this step, but interpret sharing as *telling* other people in the organisation that this is the mission (or is that vision?). And then... nothing more is heard about it, and a couple

---

[22] Quote from an interview with Ping Fu, co-founder and CEO of Geomagic, as reported in Business Life, February 2013

of years later, a new CEO comes in and starts the process again. Sounds familiar? No wonder people develop corporate deafness and a thick, cynical skin. This is not just my own cynicism speaking. Many engagement surveys report that this happens: senior teams might have great plans for the organisation and the people in it, but employees typically say they don't know about them or don't feel confident about them. The gap is created when the step of connecting with people is missed.

Sharing is partly about telling (it is the senior managers' role to set the direction), but it also involves discussion, listening and guiding as people engage with the plan and explore how it is relevant to them and the contribution they can make to achieving the goal. When we personally identify with something, we engage with it at an emotional level; when we do this, we become far more committed to the outcome. Conversely, if we don't do this, people will just continue to go about their jobs in the same way they always have done – why would they do anything else?

Make the purpose relevant

Somehow we need to make the organisational **purpose** relevant and important to each and every individual; they need to care about it. The trouble is that what may be relevant and inspiring to me, may not be relevant or inspiring to you.

Crafting the message

Susie Cranston and Scott Keller suggest that there are five essential messages to which we respond[23]: we want to know why something is important for the organisation, the customer, our team, individuals or the wider society. When we are crafting our message about a new direction and destination we need to do it in a way that speaks about all five.

---

[23] S Cranston & S Keller, *"Increasing the 'meaning quotient' of work"*, McKinsey Quarterly, Jan 2013

The pharmaceutical company Merck states the purpose of its animal health business as being about 'the science of healthier animals'. This is pretty neat: 'the science' is something individuals and teams within Merck contribute to, 'healthier animals' appeals to people concerned with the end-user (or customer) and the wider society (we all benefit from animals being healthier). And of course, if all that holds true, Merck itself will benefit.

Similarly, the construction, property and services company Kier aims "To be a world-class, customer-focused company that invests in, builds, maintains and renews the places where we live, work and play". This shows ambition (world-class), and sets out to do things ('builds, maintains and renews') that are of value to us, as employees and customers of Kier, and our community ('live, work and play').

More frequently, we come across goals and plans that fail to excite because they only speak to a narrow audience:

'Our plan is to transform M&S from a traditional British retailer into an international multi-channel retailer'. (www.marksandspencer.com)

I might be more excited about this if I worked for the firm… but then again, maybe not.

And how many companies start out with something along the lines of: 'We will be a $1bn business by 2020'.

If you had shares in the company you might be interested in this statement, but it offers very little for an employee to really grasp hold of.

A way to check the emotional strength of a goal is to PREF test it:

- **Proud:** Would you feel proud if you achieved it?
- **Respect:** What would someone you respect think if you told them this was your goal?
- **Extract:** If you took away a bit of the goal, how would you feel?
- **Fail:** If you fail to achieve it, how disappointed would you feel?

Let's apply this to the Merck example: 'We're about the science of healthier animals'. I would be proud to help animals be healthier, and am certain any expert in the field would think the same. If we were great scientists, but didn't make animals healthier, that would feel like a failure. If we failed on both counts, that would feel awful.

What about M&S's aim: to transform into an international multi-channel retailer. I have a certain pride in M&S as a British brand-name, and it's always good to see this when you go on holiday abroad, so I guess I would be proud of this bit. However, I'm not sure it would pass the 'respect' test, and would I be very upset if M&S didn't achieve this? Probably not: I don't care enough about this goal, or feel it has much to do with me whether I view it as a customer or employee.

What's it got to do with me?

So far we've talked about some of the things you can do when you're crafting the message you want to put out. If we flip that round, we also have some techniques for helping individuals find the relevance for themselves.

Kier's vision is a good example of why this is important. It stacks up pretty strongly on the PREF test: I would be **proud** to work for a world-class company and the company would command respect (personally, I would want to know why we, and others, consider ourselves to be world-class; it's a bit too easy just to claim this). If we **extract** or leave out a bit of the vision - for instance, if we didn't provide places where we lived - this would feel incomplete. Finally, if we **fail** to become world-class and build places where we live, work and play, I would feel disappointed.

However, this neatly worded vision trips off the tongue almost too easily, it doesn't make me work, I can read it passively.

I can counter this by taking a moment to really think about what these words - 'places where we live, work and play' - actually mean to me. I can conjure up my home (with a kitchen that I enjoy cooking in, a dining area big enough to have friends around for supper, a garden where my roses bloom each year), my office (with a window to daydream out of), and the park where I play with our dog. These things are really important to me; I would miss them greatly if they were no longer there.

When I think of the words 'live, work and play' in these terms – when I've reminded myself of what they mean to me, personally - my reactions to the PREF test are much stronger. I've unleashed the power of the vision because I've made it personal to me. By giving people an opportunity to bring the words of such visions to life in ways that are most meaningful to them, we can help these statements of intent gain maximum purchase. And this is precisely what the people at Kier are now in the process of doing.

Kier Group plc

When I spoke with Kier's Customer Experience Director, Jackie Ducker, we pretty quickly agreed that engaged employees are the key to delighting customers, and our conversation rapidly moved to exploring how that happens and where to start.

For Kier, it started with their customers telling them they were confused about what the company did. When they asked the people who worked for Kier 'what do you do?', customers would be told: we build hospitals OR we mend roads OR we build houses.... This came across as inconsistent and parochial, and risked customers looking for other suppliers because they didn't know how Kier could help them. In contrast, the breadth of the new vision makes it clear that Kier offers many things to many people – customers and employees alike. The statement describing what Kier does ("invests in, builds, maintains and renews the places where we live, work and play") is relevant to all.

For Jackie, getting this vision right – and securing leadership commitment to it – was the essential first step. But as she said "the words are meaningless until they become embedded and are made real".

To start this off, Kier listened to insights from its customers and employees, and followed this up with 100 people coming together from across the organisation to work out what Kier looked and felt like when it was at its best.

The words that resonated most, and that people felt made the greatest difference to customers and themselves, were 'enthusiastic, collaborative and forward thinking'. It is by showing enthusiasm, working collaboratively, and thinking ahead that the people in Kier intend to realise its vision: "To be a world-class, customer-focused company that invests in, builds, maintains and renews the places where we live, work and play".

Having established the narrative of the company's vision and how it will be achieved, Kier is now in the throes of bringing the words to life and embedding them in the fabric of the organisation. At the time of writing, this is still work-in-progress.

A series of road shows are being held to introduce the vision around the company and provide employees with an opportunity to understand and feel excited about how they can help make it happen. In addition, cross-functional teams are being set up to look at the every-day, operational activities of the business and ensure they support (and don't hinder!) enthusiastic, collaborative, forward-thinking ways of working.

Using cross-functional teams in this way has many benefits. They bring together expertise and different points of view from across organisations, ensuring richer outcomes and helping to bridge any siloes that might exist. Members of these teams also become advocates for, and role models of, the changes that are occurring, encouraging others to follow. And of course, multiple teams allow the tasks to be parcelled out in manageable lots, making the whole process less vulnerable to fatigue.

Road shows are a great place to get started. For maximum effect, they need to be interactive and give people an opportunity to work through the words themselves, rather than being passive receivers. However, as line managers we also have an opportunity to do this with our own teams.

Have a think about these two scenarios:

- **One:** I'm your boss. I hold a meeting with the team and tell you what the company has decided to do. Over four hours, I take you through a 100 slide presentation, which ends by me telling you that your goals for the year will be x, y and z, and I expect you to get on with the job.

  How enthusiastic do you feel about the company's goals? How confident do you feel about your ability to deliver? Do you feel that you make an important contribution to your organisation and that this is recognised? Do you feel inspired and motivated? What are you going to portray to your own team?

  Of course, it is difficult to imagine this scenario happening... Moving on to the second scenario.

- **Two:** I'm your boss. I gather the team and present 3 slides showing where we are as a company, the things that are causing us to make some changes, and the direction we are now embarking on. I explain what I feel about the challenge, and why I have signed up to it. We consider what we think and feel about this individually and as a team, what the new direction means to us, and how confident we feel about the contribution we can make. We hold a separate session to check our reactions and consider in more detail what we think we can achieve and how we can achieve it.

  How enthusiastic do you feel about the company's goals? How confident do you feel about your ability to deliver? Do you feel that you make a valued contribution to your organisation? Do you feel inspired and motivated? What are you going to portray to your own team?

In both cases the same information was shared, but the style was very different. In the first, I've ignored all of the motivational levers: I've removed choice from you (I've told you what to do); I haven't inspired you with the purpose because I haven't given you an opportunity to discuss why this might be important to you; and I've taken away the opportunity for you to work out what capabilities you need to apply and how to overcome any potential gaps, leaving you worried and feeling unconfident.

The second scenario is about establishing the line of sight. It takes people through a process that allows them to work out why the company's direction is important to them, and helps them work out how they can contribute to it and how they are going to go about it. This approach has the added benefit of allowing people to develop the story you've set out in a way that is meaningful to them. The fact that you are part of this conversation lends authenticity to the message, and gives you the opportunity to ensure the message remains consistent.

The MAP tool (see *Appendix: MAP tool*) is a helpful addition to the process described in the second scenario, possibly supplementing the organisation's goal setting/appraisal system. Having set out the overall goal, teams and individuals complete their MAP, answering the question: if our goal is this, what does success look like for our team/me in the next 6, 12, 24 months, and how are we/am I going to achieve it. This helps people really explore why the goal is important to them and makes the steps towards achieving it very tangible and directly relevant to their roles.

For many organisations, this cascade process means a significant commitment in terms of time and resources. There really is no substitute; it needs to happen.

Keep going: say it, be it

We have a purpose, have crafted a message that appeals on a number of fronts, have PREF-tested it and cascaded it. People identify personally with the goal and are engaged. But the process doesn't stop there. We need to continue to inspire and influence people through our on-going words, actions, decisions and behaviours: we need to say it and be it.

Say it once, say it twice, then say it again

> "What do you mean, you don't know what our goal is? I sent an email last month. I'm sure you were on the distribution list."

Because people take in information in different ways, and are often sitting in dispersed teams, the communication process (telling, discussing, listening) also has to happen through other media, over and over again, in a consistent fashion. There are a myriad of ways you can and should be communicating: the company intranet, posters, sales kick-off events, posters, mouse mats, newsletters, blogs, Chatter, recruitment criteria, appraisal criteria, conversations in the lifts or on the way into the office from the car park... Oh yes, and emails.

You will do all of this and I can guarantee that there will still be some people who will swear no-one has told them about the goal and they haven't got a clue what you're talking about. However, this group of people will become a dwindling minority – you will be well on your way to connecting with the growing majority of the people you want to take with you.

Be it

Of course, communication is not just about the words you say, print or display. It is also about how you behave. If you've decided you want to head off in a different direction, you have to 'be the change you want to see'[24].

---

[24] Attributed to Mahatma Gandhi

"I'd love to do that, really... But..."

Your organisation has decided that it exists to bring the latest innovations to your customers as quickly as possible, and that to do this you must work collaboratively both internally and with your key customers. You've gone through the process of helping people connect with and get enthusiastic about this goal: everyone knows the part they play in making the goal a reality and thinks it is important.

Then things falter.

Although the senior team set out well, when it comes down to it, they clearly do not feel comfortable about their teams sharing information with other groups, they don't release members of their team to help on cross-functional projects, and they relentlessly pursue their own results even when their decisions harm other parts of the business.

If senior managers are not prepared to change how they behave, it is unlikely that others will be persuaded to do so.

You also need to be aware of the structural barriers that exist. These are the things that support the way your team or organisation currently works. They are both a product of, and serve to underpin, your current culture. This is great if your current culture offers an environment in which people can engage and is helping you perform well. However, if it's not doing these things, it may need to change.

For instance, in the above example (*"I'd love to do that, really... But..."*), the organisation has identified it needs people to work in a more collaborative way. However, its success to date has come from being highly specialised, with different departments encouraged to become expert at what they do. Because little or no emphasis was put on departments sharing their expertise with each other, they have developed their own IT platforms and sit in different offices around the country, close to universities conducting research into their specialist areas.

If collaboration is now more highly prized than siloed expertise, these structural barriers (different IT systems and geographically dispersed teams) will need to be removed or in some way mitigated. If they are not, the teams will find it difficult to participate in collaborative innovation and projects, even if they want to. Eventually, the effort required to collaborate will dissipate and people will revert to how they've always behaved - blissfully isolated and losing market share to a rival company that does work together and brings its innovations to market more quickly.

Identifying the barriers that prevent people participating fully should form part of the initial phase of 'plotting the journey', but barriers can be difficult to spot. They are often deeply embedded in an organisation's cultural fabric. For instance, you may have an appraisal system where managers enter team member goals and ratings have to be approved by senior managers before they can be shared with the person being appraised. This may have suited a hierarchical organisation, but is less suitable for an organisation that is trying to encourage people to take more of the initiative and play a more active part in its success.

You may only start to uncover these sorts of issues when you notice that people are not engaging as you had hoped. Being alert to this danger will help. You also need to be agile and transparent in responding to these sink holes when they suddenly appear so that you can adjust the plan without derailing it.

9

Involve people

| **Involve people** | Brilliant managers | Capable people | Exercising freedom |

Let us take a step out of the office for a moment. You are walking along a road and see a cat stuck up a tree.

In the first scenario, you watch as the fire service turn up, get out a ladder, climb the tree and get the cat down. It's been an interesting thing to watch and it had a good outcome (unless you dislike cats and think this was a waste of tax-payers' money – each to their own!).

In the second scenario, you see the cat, spot a nearby ladder, get someone to hold the ladder while you overcome your fear of heights and go up it. Wobbling slightly, and holding your breath, you stretch out and grab the cat, receiving a few scratches by way of thanks. You deliver Trixie safely to her grateful owner.

In both cases, the outcome is the same: a safe, if stupid, cat. But which made your pulse race just that little bit faster (or a lot faster, if you truly don't like heights); which is the story you will still be repeating in a year's time?

I'll hazard a guess that the second scenario elicited a stronger response. Why? The rescuer got involved, overcame a challenge, did something helpful, involved other people in the task, their pulse rate went up. Many of these things appear in our list of 'highly engaged' characteristics (see How do engaged and disengaged people behave?). This is what this final step is about: getting people involved.

So far our process for engaging people has concentrated on establishing and sharing a **purpose**. This final stage focuses on ensuring people are equipped to participate to the full extent of their abilities (**capable**) and have the freedom to apply those skills (**control**).

Brilliant managers

The first essential ingredient is Brilliant Managers (by which I also mean Brilliant Leaders). At the risk of repetition, you cannot force someone to be engaged. While managers could and should set an expectation that people will engage fully, their most important contribution comes from creating an environment where people feel able to engage fully.

As a manager or leader, your role essentially is there to facilitate: to aid people making progress in their roles, through catalysts (actions that support the activities being undertaken) and nourishers (recognition, support and encouragement of the person); and to minimise inhibitors and toxins (the obstacles and the things that disengage us). [25]

Some of this is basic good management. Rather than go into great depth on these subjects I've concentrated on bringing out a few salient pointers that might help with the task of creating engaging environments, grouped into the following topics:

- You
- Inspiring, trusted, authentic communicator of the 'why'
- Creator of opportunities

---

[25] TM Amabile & SJ Kramer, *"The Power of Small Wins"*, Harvard Business Review, May 2011

- Proficient operator
- Celebrator of progress
- Culture builder

The references and reading list at the end of the book offer some suggestions of where you might want to go for more detail; as with other chapters, I've also included some short case studies to show how various organisations have approached some of these things in very practical ways.

The first of these case studies comes courtesy of Liz Ellis, HR Director for Danone Baby Nutrition (UK). It heads up this section because their experience covers so much of what this book is recommending[26].

Danone Baby Nutrition (UK)

Danone is a large, multinational company with a string of best-selling consumer brands. However, while they are a big company with over 100,000 employees worldwide, they have adopted a business model that gives local business units considerable autonomy to build and drive their parts of the organisation as they see fit. People are given a clear purpose, framework and expectations, and are then given the freedom to use their strengths to good effect.

HR Director Liz Ellis puts some of their success down to the size of the business unit (~250 people), which allows people to remain in touch with each other and come together around a defined purpose. People maintain personal connections; they can see what they are responsible for as a team and individually, and can see the direct effects of their actions.

Teamwork is crucial to this business, as is the emphasis on using strengths and being dissatisfied with the status quo (individuals and teams regularly use the Stop, Start, Do Differently technique).

---

[26] The SKS (Stop, Keep Doing, Start) process is widely accredited to Professor Phil Daniels of Brigham Young University

Their appraisal system affords behaviours as much weight as outcomes, as does their reward and recognition scheme 'Do You Dare To Dream', which has helped to develop a culture of people 'dreaming the impossible stuff', and applying it to both their personal lives and their work.

When I asked Liz what her advice would be to other organisations keen on developing an environment where high engagement is the norm she offered three suggestions:

1. Have daily, one-to-one interactions with people.

2. Find a way to get the business to take engagement seriously.

3. Continue to nurture: e.g. by calling out behaviours that are not helpful; by giving feedback; by having safe havens where people can let off steam and regroup.

You

Without exception, every set of engagement survey results I've ever seen has shown that our immediate managers or leaders have a significant impact on whether we feel engaged or not.

Take a moment to test that:

Managers I've liked/disliked		
	Liked	Didn't like
What did you like/dislike about them?		
How did this affect your performance?		

How engaged did you feel while you worked for them?		

Then extend this to yourself:

How does my behaviour affect others?	
How does my behaviour hinder others?	
What will I do to change this?	
How does my behaviour help others?	
What will I do to enhance this?	

If you as a leader or manager are that important to the engagement mix, there are three things you need to be brilliant at:

1. *Being a role model* by making a personal choice to engage and demonstrating it. This gives you the authority to set expectations that people are there to perform and participate to the best of their ability - turning up is not enough.

2. *Knowing yourself* so that you use your strengths to the maximum and can adapt superbly to others. Remember those letters – ENTJ or ISFP – what did they mean on the last MBTI®[27]

---

[27] Myers-Briggs Type Indicator

you did? And what was that colour you came out as in the Insight Discovery® profile? Dust off the personality, behavioural and preference assessments that you have sitting in a draw somewhere and check what they say about how you prefer to be and how you might behave when you're experiencing stress. You can also check the profiles of your team members and see how you might best work together and how you could flex towards others who have different preferences[28].

3. *Not demotivating or disengaging the people around you:* This tends to happen inadvertently rather than intentionally, either because the managers concerned don't nurture their people sufficiently or don't know them well enough to put their trust in them and therefore don't given them the freedom to get on with their jobs. This can also happen when managers, acting out of a misguided belief that they are helping, rush into situations to solve problems rather than helping someone solve the problem for themselves.

Inspiring, trusted, authentic communicator of the 'why'

A lot of this was covered in the chapter on *Connect with people*. Essentially it is about knowing how to explain the 'why', in a manner that is authentic to you and inspiring to others, and then being consistent as you repeat the message across the various media (from posters and emails to coffee shop encounters and formal meetings). Your consistent message also needs to be evident in your behaviour, the decisions you take and the direction you set for people.

Bear in mind that the most effective form of communication is one-to-one, face-to-face. When we are in this setting our verbal and body language are working optimally: we can check understanding, adjust our method of delivery and tailor our message to appeal directly to the person in front of us.

---

[28] A recommended read on behavioral preferences: R Bolton & D Grover Bolton "*Social Style/Management Style: Developing Productive Work Relationships*", 1984

However, in the real world, other things often get in the way and we may find ourselves having to use the phone, Skype, email etc., and often communicating with more than one person at a time. All of these things get in the way of delivering meaning and prevent our message from being understood as we intended. These are not excuses; they are the realities of our everyday lives and they mean you have to work harder and be more conscious of how you're communicating in order to be effective.

Being authentic is of course a personal recipe. Your leader at work might be energetic, gregarious, calm or shy. All 'types' of people can make good leaders, but we tend to respond better to them when we know they are being true to themselves and their own characters, not trying to be something they are not. That said, there are some things that people seem to like to see in their leaders and colleagues: the 'universal truths' of honesty, fairness, respect and integrity[29].

Honesty

Tell things as they are - the good, the bad, and the ugly[30]. In one company I worked with, the managing director pushed me to do this when feeding back the verbatim comments from an engagement survey to the assembled UK company. As well as the 'everything is great' comments, we also put up the more humbling ones such as: 'The leadership team are stunningly out of touch with what is going on in the business'. Apart from the sharp intake of breath from the audience, the effect was to lend truth and perspective to all the comments (good, bad, or ugly) and open the channel for more frank conversations in the weeks that followed.

---

[29] R Bolton & D Grover Bolton *"Social Style/Management Style: Developing Productive Work Relationships"*, 1984; just as a check: how many of these appear on the 'value posters' that sit on the walls of your organisation?

[30] For some readers, this will immediately trigger the evocative theme tune to Sergio Leone's 1966 film 'The Good, The Bad & The Ugly' – I make no apologies for putting that into your head for the rest of the day, it's a good message to remember.

Fairness

We look for fairness in many things. One of the most emotive is pay, where it is often confused with the issue of equality. In many engagement surveys there is a question about pay. Regardless of the words used, the reader typically reads the question as: "Do you think you are paid enough?" Unsurprisingly, most people tend to say "no", particularly if they think (rightly or wrongly) that other people are getting paid more than them. However, the topic of pay and compensation is often then ignored in the post-survey conversations: it feels too hard and many managers duck the issue by saying pay has nothing to do with them, it is out of their hands.

That might be true, but all managers should be able to explain pay policy. Hopefully, they can enlighten people on the concept that the organisation may not pay everyone the same (because we have different experience and levels of responsibility etc.) but does treat people fairly (promotions or increments are agreed in a transparent way, free of bias). If this isn't the case in your organisation, you need to be influencing the senior leadership team to ensure this is put right. I don't say this just because fairness is a strong personal value, but because this can derail teams and organisations if left unattended. Unfairness is a canker.

Treating people with respect

Actions often speak louder than words with this one (beware the "With respect..." start to a sentence... it usually means the opposite). For instance, we usually employ people because we think they are capable of doing something. It is respectful to then allow them to use their expertise and to listen to their opinions. We may then choose not to act on that opinion, but hopefully only after taking it into consideration and explaining this to the person concerned.

Integrity

Demonstrate clearly that you consistently do what you say you will do. This is short and sweet, but often pretty hard to do.

One more attribute we might add to the list is courage. This came up in a number of the interviews I did for this book, and is perhaps particularly valuable when things are not going well, or there are difficult decisions to be made and the way ahead is foggy.

I suspect courage, like motivation, comes in all forms and from all sources. If you don't already know your own 'courage triggers', it may be useful to reflect on a time when you showed courage or took a courageous decision:

Reflecting on courage	
What were the circumstances that required you to be courageous?	
What did it feel like? What made it feel different?	
What steps did you take to get to get to the outcome you wanted?	
How will you approach a similar challenge in the future?	

Creator of opportunities

If you are keen to create an environment where people automatically participate and contribute, you need to become a master at both spotting opportunities to get people involved and at stepping back, giving people space to contribute in a way that makes the most of their strengths. That's not an invitation to pass the buck or do less; it frees you to do more with some of the other parts of your role.

Command & control   Interdependent collaboration

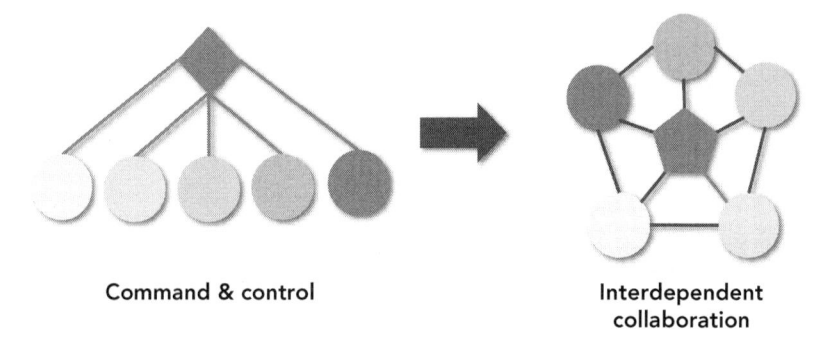

Figure 11: Towards interdependent collaboration

It also allows you to move from a command & control type of set up, where everyone is working as individuals as you direct them, through to one where people are inter-dependent on each other and collaborating without the need for your coordination.

Goal setting presents a great opportunity to involve people. What did your heart just do when you read those words 'goal setting': groan or leap for joy…

There is a very apt section on goal setting in K2's book 'Perform' and how it can be useful and motivating but is often abused.[31] In business, goals are generally pretty useful: they help to focus the mind, provide a framework for decision-making, and signal when you've achieved what you set out to do. When used well they are also excellent tools

---

[31] K Hatter, C Shambrook, J Constable, K Grainger, *"Perform"*, Dec 2013

for helping people feel part of what's going on; when they are misused they can quickly demotivate!

Lots of organisations do an annual downward cascade of goals: 'This is what the company wants to achieve: 10% sales growth, and a profit margin of 40%. Because you work for this company, these are also your goals'.

While employees certainly need to be doing things that contribute to the overall company goal (that's what you pay them for), this sort of goal doesn't work particularly well for individuals. Is the company really going to hold each person accountable for achieving 10% sales growth and a 40% margin? There is a very real danger that this will feel unreachable for most people and disconnected from both their roles and personal areas of control.

In the rugby ball model of engagement, this is equivalent to severing the link between the individual and the organisation:

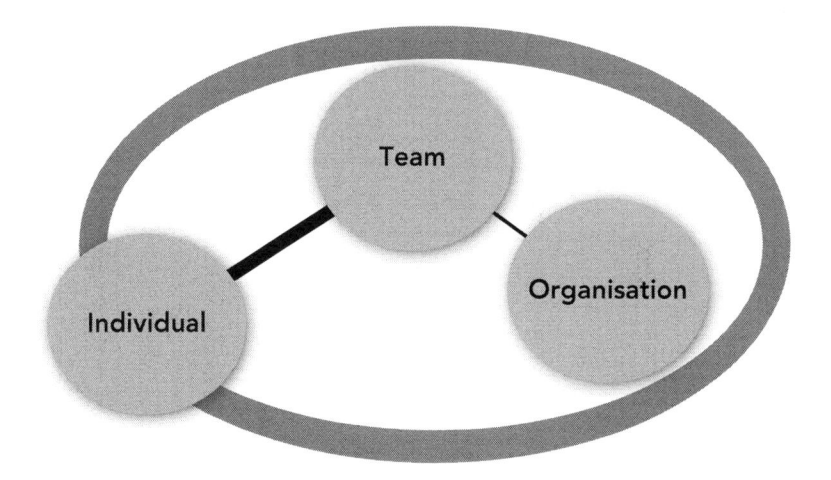

Figure 12: Severing the links

I've been generous here and suggested the individual is still strongly attached to their team, but that would be a happy coincidence and the result of habit rather than anything else. It is far less likely that the activities of individuals are benefitting the organisation they work for; indeed because they are not properly focused and aligned, many of the things they spend their time doing will probably either have no positive effect for the organisation or will be detrimental.

Let's rerun how it might look if we involve people: this is where 'top down' meets 'bottom up' and expands in the middle, and is similar to the techniques discussed in the chapter *Connect with people*.

- **Top down:** We still have an overall aim for the organisation (possibly a rolling three-year plan, with a one year sharper focus, appealing to people's sense of present and future).

- **Bottom up:** People from across the organisation have been involved in coming up with the target before it is announced (and it still reflects their input!). The target benefits from their expertise (lending it veracity) and the dynamic of stretch (see *Exercising freedom*): the target feels challenging but attainable.

- **Expanding middle:** You get your team together to take them through the goals and you give your view of where you think you need to be focused. You ask for input on the team's goals from members of the team and ask them to consider the implications for their own goals.

This isn't an invitation to create mayhem – the people who work for you are not idiots or children. Because you have set the context, shown ownership of your bit of the total picture, and invited the people who work with you to contribute and identify what this means for their individual goals, you have far greater buy-in from the start, and therefore a far greater prospect of realising the outcomes you're aiming for.

When people really get into the swing of this, they start to identify where their individual goals are dependent on others and vice versa, first within their immediate functional teams and then wider. This is a good way of bridging silos[32] and achieving the seeming mathematical impossibility where the whole is greater than the sum of the parts.

I saw at first hand the power of this method of goal setting within certain functions at D&B and was further convinced by Jane Miller, HR Director at Severn Trent Water. Speaking at a Vybrant event, she described how the utility company had used this method of goal setting to help build an environment where people understood and owned their bit of delivering what they hoped was exceptional customer service. When your product is water, and it is taken as a given that it will be clean and available, the biggest differentiator between competing providers is the quality of the service they offer, particularly when things go wrong. Service is delivered through people. To do this well they had to have the skills, know-how and when to apply them, and care about the difference they make to the end user. This isn't about board-room visions, it's about everyday, real activities.

Proficient operator

Much of your job as a manager or leader in a business is to use your influence to remove obstacles from your team's path and then get out of their way! If you've recruited people with the right skills and aptitude, given them the right amount of responsibility and freedom, and set the context and overall aims out clearly, they will achieve what you ask of them and more. Of course, things rarely go completely as expected, so be on hand to help them adjust as conditions change.

An operational tool that is perhaps over used, but that you nevertheless need to be highly proficient at, is the art of conducting effective

---

[32] The word 'silo' has taken on a lot of negative connotations, conjuring up organisational units that somehow shut themselves off from the rest of the world and acquire hermit-like status. If we reclaim the word and instead think of silos as towers of expertise, small enough for the experts within to exercise control, and often operating highly efficiently, then the concept of silos becomes easier to acknowledge. In this view of the world, silos are not as detrimental as we might have thought, and rather than finding ways to break them down (as a lot of current wisdom suggests) we might find it more fruitful to build bridges to connect them.

meetings. They have various primary functions: information sharing, decision-making etc. However, because they are by definition a meeting of people they also present a myriad of opportunities to involve people... or to disengage and supremely annoy!

There are shelves full of books on this subject (and some very good John Cleese management training videos if you are of my generation!). A quick check-list that might suffice:

- What is the meeting for? A clear agenda will help others to understand their roles in the meeting and the desired outcome.
- Who needs to be in the meeting and what roles do they have?
- What content is being shared before, during and after the meeting?
- What do they need to do before, during and after the meeting: is the meeting about sharing information, exploring ideas, and/or making decisions?
- How will you ensure people are able to participate effectively?
- How will you encourage participation ahead of, during and after the meeting?
- Where are you meeting (location, virtual) and for how long: what practicalities do you need to pay attention to in order for the meeting to be successful in its outcome and method?
- How will you know whether the meeting has been successful: where did you get to on your MAP, what was the feedback, did people do what was required?

Stop a moment. We've probably all read or been told before about how to run effective meetings and my guess is we still don't get it right. Are we just being consciously incompetent?

Yes. Possibly because effective meetings aren't actually about checklists, but are instead about behaviours. If this isn't how we currently behave, it will take conscious effort to change, and this is likely to feel laborious and uncomfortable before we get to the point when these things have become a habit.

When I approach a behavioural change, I've learnt that I'm more successful if I just concentrate on one thing at a time; even then it is usually months before I realise the new behaviour has become habit.

Consider the following:

Participative meetings	
What one thing are you going to focus on to ensure people fully participate in your meetings?	
How would you rate yourself on this at the moment?	
How will you know this has improved?	

Celebrator of progress

Recognise individuals and teams in a way that is of value to those people. If you don't know what that is, ask them. Indeed, if you don't have any reward and recognition practices in your organisation or team, this is a great opportunity to get people involved – ask them what they think should be recognised (behaviours as well as outcomes) and what they would value as a reward. This is also not just about you thanking your team: it is about everyone being able to thank anyone who has made a difference – if that's what they choose to do!

A couple of scenarios that may feel familiar:

- You've had a stellar year and made a significant contribution to your organisation's profits. Your boss is feeling very generous and rewards you with a slap-up meal at a top London restaurant, with an overnight stay in a 5-star hotel. Very nice and you appreciate the gesture. But what you would really love is a few extra days holiday with your husband and your kids who you haven't spent much time with in the last few months….

- You have a number of team members who've been delivering great customer service in the past month. You get the whole team together and hand out bottles of champagne to those who've gone above and beyond. They all appreciate the 'thank you' and recognition, but a couple of them don't actually drink…. Some alternatives might have been speciality chocolates, cinema tickets, book tokens, magazine subscriptions or an Elgin Football Club hat. The key is that if you can reward people with something they value (like the hat!), you magnify the effect of the thank you.

With a bit of thought and tailoring we could have made both gestures so much more powerful for the people involved.

When you're thinking about recognising people or teams, don't wait for just the big things to land. Take time to celebrate progress, not just final results; this also gives you an opportunity to review and adjust, and to make this a normal part of how you work. Also look to make the links to the behaviours that differentiate your business and provide you with competitive edge; Danone's 'Dare to Dream' reward and recognition platform does exactly that (see *Danone Baby Nutrition (UK)*).

Culture builder

Even if you are not at the top of your organisation, you have a strong influence on the culture in your immediate vicinity. There are many books and thoughts on culture. The description that makes most sense to me is to view culture as 'the way things are done around here'. It encompasses how we make decisions, how we behave towards one another, what values we demonstrate (not just talk about), and what we choose to do and not do[33].

Because you, as a manager or leader in a business, make decisions, behave in a certain way and demonstrate the things that are important to you through the choices you make, you play a key part in building the culture in your bit of the organisation. And because you really are that powerful, you need to be skilled at (and mindful of) building a culture that encourages and supports people to participate to the maximum. The cultures that don't do this suggest it is not a straightforward or easy task.

On-boarding

A very practical consideration is how you on-board people, and this can apply whether we are talking about just one person joining an organisation or an entire workforce joining as a result of a merger. In organisations of any size, a good on-boarding process is crucial in helping your new recruits become effective quicker. But again, it is easy to miss, do badly, or not get quite right.

One large company I've come across is in a growth phase and is rapidly bringing in new people. It has spent a lot of money on ensuring all new recruits are aware of the company history, the ethos, the hierarchy, and the activities. However, it wasn't as punctilious about making sure its new recruits had transport, a computer or a phone. The experience inspired and frustrated with equal measure, delaying integration with the organisation and raising doubts about the business's competency.

---

[33] Recommended reading on this: G Johnson & K Scholes *"Exploring Corporate Strategy"*, 1993 (particularly on the Cultural Web) and C Taylor, *"Walking the Talk: Building a Culture for Success"*, 2005

Getting on-boarding right is particularly important in medium to large-sized companies, where it is easier for new recruits to miss out on things that will help them get up to speed easily; in smaller companies, it is easy to ask the person sat next to you. Although it can be the little things that trip people up initially, these do eventually get sorted out. The longer-term success of a new recruit (or merged workforce) is often more critically influenced by how they are introduced into the culture of their new organisation and their subsequent experience of how things work.

They will already have certain expectations of you derived from their recruitment: from the way the job advert was phrased and the conditions attached, to the interview process and the stories portrayed of the organisation's past and future. Up to this point, these interactions tend to telegraph the culture you say you want (though not always – it is worth checking occasionally). Once the new recruit has joined you, their experience of your culture – the actual way you do things – is often at odds with what you purport to be: the internal brand gap. This matters because:

1. It will take the new recruit longer to work out how to behave in your organisation if you don't actually do what you say you do. This means it will take them longer to be effective.

2. If they can't adapt (because they thought they were joining a place that behaved in a different way), they are likely to leave. This is expensive for you and them, both in terms of recruitment costs and wasted time.

Even if the internal brand gap is small (you mostly act in the way you said you would act), you will need to invest time and effort in helping your new recruits get to grips with the every-day implications of your culture and adjust (it is unlikely they are perfectly aligned with the organisation's culture to start with).

The following case study shows the importance of on-boarding in a rapidly growing company.

Passing on your company DNA

Operating in the fast moving world of technology, this company has grown exponentially in little more than a decade from an idea to a medium-sized, international company employing over 500 people. The tipping point for the company came in 2012-13, when they reached the 250-employee mark. The company realised that the rapid pace of expansion in staff numbers was putting the company's DNA at risk, with the new recruits (many at a senior level) diluting not only what had made the company successful so far, but what the executive team also saw as being important for them in the future.

With this realisation, the company invested time and money in their on-boarding process, allowing people to experience, assimilate and align with the company's DNA. Indeed, when I interviewed a senior director at the company and asked what his one piece of advice would be for other companies, it was to "get the on-boarding right, but understand it takes time and it takes longer than you think." Key to this process was to ensure that everyone in the organisation (the people going through the on-boarding process, their colleagues, their managers) understood the process and had the right expectations: "Give people time to take everything on board and then they will be productive in the way you recognise; leaders must avoid being too impatient to get to this point."

There are of course many other things that are inextricably linked to your role in building environments where people can engage to the maximum. Some of these are considered later in this book (see *Some specific applications*). You also have a part to play in the next two topics: ensuring people are highly capable and have the freedom to exercise these capabilities.

Capable people

Because this book is looking at life from the perspective of a manager or leader, I've narrowed down this wide topic to three dimensions:

1. You as a leader or manager of the business, making assessments about what skills and capabilities are required for the organisation to be successful now and in the years to come.

2. You as a developer of people, helping them to gain and use the skills that make the most of their strengths and mitigate their weaknesses.

3. You as a contributor to the success of the organisation, ensuring your own capabilities are the best they can be and being used well.

As this entire book is about you as a contributor, this section focuses on the first two dimensions.

You as a strategic leader of the business

The first area – you as a leader of the business - affects the entire employee lifecycle: from recruitment, through on-boarding and on-going development, to exiting people when their talents or attitudes no longer fit what the organisation now needs.

Conducting a gap analysis is a good place to start (see Appendix: Gap Analysis). This involves looking at your collective skill levels (depth and breadth) and deciding whether these are sufficient or not. If they are not sufficient, you need to work out how to address the gap; if they are sufficient, you need to make sure they remain that way (all skills can go rusty or become obsolete as things around us change – being able to type on a typewriter was useful in the past but is less so now).

We can also add in a time dimension, aligned with the company's vision and strategy. What skills will you need to be successful in 3/5/10 years time? Often this will be an organic evolution from where you are now, but if it isn't obvious take a look outside your organisation: ask your customers what they will expect from you in the future; see what your competitors are doing; or find out more about world-class leaders in other industries that you would want to emulate.

Once these attributes are identified, you can assess how good you are at them now and draw up plans to promote any strengths and address any shortfalls (e.g. through training and developing the people you've got, recruitment of new talent, and of course practise, practise, practise). This needs to happen with as much diligence as you put into ensuring your products, processes, IT system, etc. are fit for purpose.

Recruitment
Developing the people you've already got is the subject of the next section but before moving on, just a bit more on recruitment. We looked at the importance of on-boarding in Culture builder, and noted that the recruitment process provides your new recruits with their first taste of your true culture. It also offers you your first chance to bring in the type of people you believe will make you, your team and/or your organisation successful. This boils down to two things:

1. What competencies they need to have to be successful now.

2. What qualities will ensure they are successful in your organisation in the future.

Competencies is about looking for specific skills (brick laying, dentistry, cooking, copy writing) and evidence that they can be applied well (can the person follow a process, solve problems, coordinate with others and communicate). Qualities are about attitude, adaptability and agility; things that are both useful now and suggest that the person's skills will still be relevant in a few years time.

There is some artistry required in formulating the ideal 'recipe for success', but it doesn't all have to be guesswork. You could look at successful people in your organisation or industry and draw up a picture of the sort of competencies and qualities they have. Although useful, this technique comes with a warning: sometimes it is useful to recruit people who break the current mould. They may make uncomfortable waves, but they can often bring new perspectives and may have the exact qualities you need for the future when conditions are different.

Having identified the set of competencies and qualities you want, you can now make sure your recruitment process not only asks that candidates demonstrate these attributes but also mirrors them. If you are looking for creative people, make your recruitment process creative. If you are looking for analytical people, make it analytical. If you are looking for people who care about the service they provide others, make sure your recruitment process screams 'care'.

By way of an example, take a look at the recruitment pages on the website for Ask, the Italian restaurant chain. Ask puts Italian passion at the heart of what they do. The words literally appeal to the cuore and spirito (heart and soul) and presumably are designed to attract people who demonstrate the same level of emotional energy and verve.

You've just been given some extra budget and want to recruit for a new position in your team:

Recruiting for success	
How will you identify what competencies you are looking for now?	
What are the key attributes you are looking for?	

Will they need to have different competencies in 3 years time? If yes, what qualities will you look for in the candidate that will help to ensure they remain successful in the future?	
What will the candidates experience during the recruitment process? How will that help them and you make a good decision?	

You as a developer of people

When given the opportunity to develop people, apply the same rigour you would when recruiting. Refresh your memory of a person's CV or their details on your company's talent management system, canvass opinions from other people they interact with as they may see a side to the person in question that you haven't seen. Most of all involve the person you are helping to develop: ask about their past experiences and aspirations. Armed with all of this information you will be in a much better position to identify possible development paths and opportunities for people that fit the organisation's trajectory.

Many managers report they would like to do more to develop their people but lack the funding. While we can learn much through experience gained on the job, this takes time and often fails to develop people to their full potential. I would argue that having highly capable, engaged people is increasingly becoming the differentiator between competing firms and that you can help sharpen this competitive advantage by funding appropriate training, mentoring and coaching programmes that help your staff get to and remain at the top of their games.

Of course, you also have a part to play as trainer, mentor and coach. Many of us are thrown into the task of leading or managing a team with little training on how to develop the people that now report to us. Two pieces of advice: first, go on at least one good course to teach you how to coach and put what you learn into practice; and second, at some point in your career, seek a move into a team where you are the leader but also the least technically proficient person in the team. As well as being a humbling experience, this is a fantastic environment in which to hone your coaching skills – all you can do is ask questions; you don't have the option of slipping into 'telling' or 'advising' mode.

As a very quick checklist (and hoping my own coach, Deni Lyall, doesn't wince too much at my reductionism), here are some specifics to think about when you are acting as a coach (helping someone solve their own problems) or mentor (advising, perhaps based on how you tackled a similar problem in the past) to your team or colleagues[34]:

- **Questioning skills:** using open, clean, rich questions for exploring issues (e.g. tell me about, what happened next, how did that help) and closed questions for decisions (e.g. are you going to do that). Check you're not talking too much, or leading the performer (you might think it's helpful but it's actually really irritating – if you've got a point to make, just say it then get back to being a coach).

- **CALIBRE listening:**
  ☐ Concentrate on what's being said (and not said)
  ☐ Acknowledge and clarify to check your understanding
  ☐ Leave room for silence
  ☐ Interest – show this through your posture and listen out for unusual statements or words
  ☐ Be in the room – get rid of other distractions

---

[34] See the references at the end for some of the books I've found most useful in my own training as a coach, particularly the books by Sue Knight, Carol Wilson and John Whitmore

- ☐ Response – suggest options based on what you've heard (not what you would necessarily do) and listen to the answer before thinking of the next question
- ☐ Evaluate – be aware of your assumptions and tone down the value & experience filters you will be applying

- **Adapting & attitude:** shifting your style closer to the person being coached and be prepared to adopt different techniques depending on the attitude of the performer. Maintaining an attitude of curiosity and appropriate level of tenacity.

- **STAMP – a checklist for the practicalities of coaching:**
  - ☐ What **skills** will you use? – e.g. what's the opening question?
  - ☐ What **time** is needed? – e.g. try to avoid back-to-back meetings
  - ☐ What's the **agenda**? – e.g. are you coaching someone around something specific? where have you got to in the process?
  - ☐ Are you prepared in **mind & body**? – e.g. are you ready to listen?
  - ☐ Where are you going to coach? – e.g. we often work in goldfish bowls, is that the appropriate **place** for this session?

- **Learning cycle:** we all have certain preferences for how we learn, but the process usually follows the pattern of plan, perform and review (see *Figure 13: Learning cycle*). We often focus on the perform bit of this, but without reviewing the effect of our actions and planning to do something different if we are not achieving the outcome we want, will just perpetuate the same thing over an over. We also have an opportunity to learn when we do achieve what we wanted: what helped us to do this; how are we going to replicate that and do it even faster next time or more consistently? Adding the review and plan parts to the cycle allow us to learn and adapt and it is your role as a developer of people to help them do this, including by giving people the space to make mistakes and try something different.

> "I'm always doing that which I cannot do, in order that I may learn how to do it" - Picasso

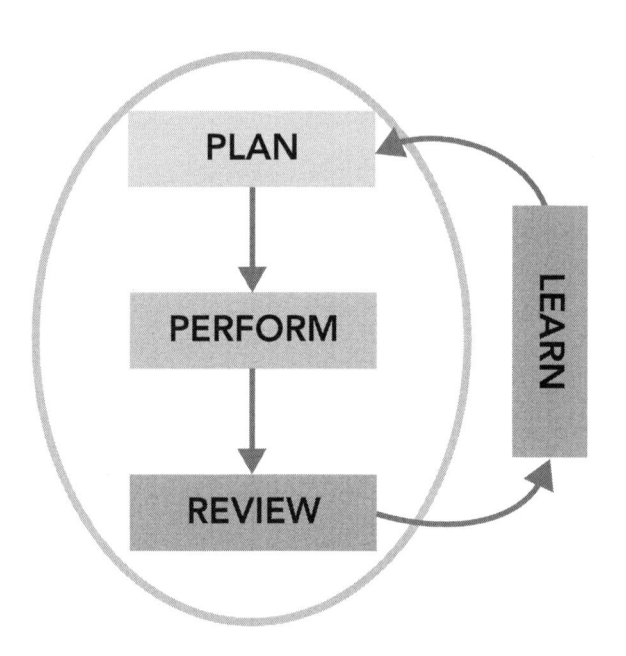

Figure 13: Learning cycle

Owning my own development

Although this book is primarily about what you can do as a manager or leader to help create engaging environments, individuals within the organisation also carry a responsibility both to contribute to that environment and to choose to participate. This includes individuals taking responsibility for developing their own skills and applying them with confidence so that they are able to participate to the full extent of their abilities.

People most notably think about this when they are considering how to progress their careers – or rather how their boss is going to progress their career for them. A lot of engagement surveys ask whether people are satisfied with the help they get to develop their careers, and judging from the results, many people aren't.

This is a powerful example of where engagement surveys get stuck in perpetuating parent-child behaviours. The survey question often effectively says: "Because you've joined this organisation to do x, the organisation is now responsible for your progression to do y or z. Are you happy with how you are progressing?" This invites the response: "Oh it's your fault I haven't got a better paid job is it? No, I'm not happy!" Does that sound familiar?

As managers in an organisation it is in our interests that people develop their skills so that they perform well. It makes sense therefore that we should support people in achieving this, for instance by giving people time to study, arranging for secondments and project work to widen their experience or finding funding for a certain course. However, my team member's career is not my career, it is theirs; it is theirs to develop it as they see fit, to achieve the things they want to achieve.

I'm hoping the environment you work in is already one where you are helped to achieve the things you want, with the onus for developing your career clearly sitting with you. If you don't operate in that sort of place yet, and you don't actually want to be responsible for the careers of everyone around you, what are the things you can encourage that could bring about a shift?

This is where mindset, attitude and expectations come in. A good starting place is to have a conversation where you clearly set expectations that individuals own their career development and that your role is to support them. In the case of mindset and attitude, these are two of the cornerstones of engagement, and like engagement, you can't do either for someone else. Just because you want someone to be more positive, tenacious, curious or willing to learn does not mean it will happen. However, you can have conversations with people that open their minds to the effect (good and bad) their mindset and attitude has on the task in hand and the people around them, and the fact that they have a choice about the mindset and attitude they adopt.[35]

Exercising freedom

People generally feel more motivated when they have some say in what they do and how they do it – i.e. they have some degree of freedom to decide. While we occasionally like to be told what to do (maybe because we lack the experience or the energy to work it out for ourselves), this can become frustrating when it is prolonged: we become fed up and cease to participate.

As a manager or leader in a business our role is to provide people with the context and parameters, and be there to support them as they use their expertise to address the issue at hand. We've already encountered a couple of tools that can help us in this: the MAP (Must, Aspire, Phenomenal) and HIC (Help, Impact, Control) tool. The first helps people work out what they are aiming for and the tactics they are going to use; the second helps them assess their choices and prioritise (see *Appendix: MAP tool; Appendix: HIC tool – Help, Impact, Control*).

Of course the point here is that, as leaders, we are helping our team members come to these realisations themselves. We can help in two ways:

1. Coaching, supporting, removing barriers: i.e. being *Brilliant managers*.

---

[35] The people at Planet K2 are masters at helping people to understand about choice. A recommended read is *"Perform"* by K Hatter, C Shambrook, J Constable, K Grainger, Dec 2013

2. Setting the context and overall aim, then getting people involved in working out their part in delivering a successful outcome.

We started looking at the second topic in the section on being a *Creator of opportunities*. The following scenario looks at that in a bit more detail. We start with a mainly top-down goal-setting process that has allowed some tailoring at a functional level.

> "We want to be the number one in the UK in terms of market share and we're going to do that by growing our key customers, working through distributors for our smaller customers, and investing in our technology platforms and customer service experience. I am the Customer Services Manager and my part of this is to ensure we are delivering an industry-leading customer service experience for our key clients. Given this, your role is to deliver a great service and meet these targets for call times and volumes and achieve a customer satisfaction score of 65%. You'll do it by answering queries in this way, with this information."

> Team member: "It's clear. I know what's expected of me. But I haven't had any input in setting the goal. Where did my manager get the figure of 65% from? Is this something I'm happy to sign up to? Is this something that will make good use of my strengths? These are just questions buzzing around in my head, as I haven't been invited to comment or contribute."

Let's rewrite the last bit of that (wouldn't that be great if we could actually do that in our day jobs).

> "We want to be the number one in the UK in terms of market share, and we're going to do that by growing our key customers, working through distributors for our smaller customers and investing in our technology platforms and customer service experience. As the Customer Services

Manager my part of this is to ensure we are delivering an industry-leading customer service experience for our key customers. Given our team strengths and what our competitors are delivering, I think we should be aiming for a two-second answer time and a customer satisfaction score of 65% as a minimum. In your role as a customer services agent, what do you think of this objective and how could you help us achieve it?"

Team member: "We have some pretty good responses that help our customers quickly and effectively but not all of our team are confident with them. One of my strengths is one-to-one training. I'll spend an hour a day bringing everyone up to scratch with this and ask Jo to do the same as she is also a good trainer. If we're all using these responses and are feeling more confident, I think we could get to a customer satisfaction score of 70%."

Sounds too good to be true? I've paraphrased the conversation a bit, but this is a scenario I've witnessed. The outcome was a customer satisfaction score of over 70%, and a highly engaged team that the following year set the bar even higher. Stretch becomes a regular part of life with engaged people who are given the freedom to exercise their capabilities.

Many managers will already be doing this regularly, and some will always consider it unnecessary (though the latter are probably not the type to read this book). For those who perhaps see the benefit in this approach, but are not using it, what is causing you to hesitate or preventing you from taking this approach?

There could be some very practical reasons. For instance, the top-down cascade happens so slowly you are already well into the year in question when the objectives get to you – there isn't time to invite people to participate in the process. Or, the company engages people in a bottom-up goal-setting process but then what subsequently gets cascaded from the top seems to bear no relation to this. People feel their input has been dismissed and the resulting targets are nothing to do with them.

I could argue that these are excuses or that you should be influencing upward to get the conditions changed, but a more practical suggestion would be to get people as involved as you can in the timeframes available and acknowledge that the process is not perfect.

I have also heard some other objections to getting people involved in setting their own goals or participating in the goal setting process.

- *"Some of the people in my team just don't get it and would set themselves ridiculously easy goals"*. Have you really taken the time to explain the context and expectations to them, in a way they can understand? If you have, and they still don't 'get it', it could be they lack the experience or confidence to set realistic goals, so you could try meeting them half way with some guidance, or sharing the goals of similarly placed people. If you really run out of options, you have possibly recruited the wrong people into your team.

- *"It's my role to shield my team from everything happening above; they don't need to worry about all that corporate stuff"*. In effect you are saying: "whatever else is going on, it's nothing to do with us, we'll just do what we've always done". This might shield your team from feeling angst, but you run the risk that someone will one day decide what you're doing isn't benefitting the company anymore and stops it. Have the courage to explain what the organisation is doing and invite people to find a way to connect and contribute to it.

- *"I don't feel comfortable with the direction the company's going in, so I'm just going to ignore it; we'll keep doing our own thing"*. This situation doesn't become less awkward because you avoid talking about it. Seek clarification upwards, find something you can focus on and acknowledge there are uncertainties – the people in your team can deal with this.

Exercising freedom has two sides to it: it involves the manager making room for people to make choices and implement decisions within a given contextual framework; and it involves the team member having the skills, confidence and attitude to put this freedom to good effect.

Take a few minutes to think about an approaching task:

Creating space	
How could you get your team more involved in this task?	
What would be the benefits of getting them involved?	
What's stopping you? How can you get rid of these barriers?	

10

Some specific applications

The intention has been to make this book practical in its application. The following chapters look at three topics where engagement (people participating fully) is vital to success:

- Taking people with you through change
- Developing effective virtual teams
- Building profitable, long-lasting customer relationships

The topics themselves – managing change, teams and customers – are vast and there are many books and articles dedicated to each of them. I have assumed you've either read some of these and/or have experienced the subjects first hand, and that we can concentrate instead on some of the techniques that could help foster engagement as you undertake these activities.

Even then these chapters are not exhaustive or meant to be the last word on these subjects; indeed I hope they spark further questions and ideas as you read through them.

Taking people with you through change

The truism is true: "change is a constant". Heraclitus said this some 2.5 thousand years ago and many of us would agree that the speed of change is accelerating in pace and scope.

We have all experienced change. We might have chosen it (getting married, having children, taking a new job, moving house, changing our diet) or it may have come unbidden (ill-health, redundancy, divorce). It might have been straightforward (a decision involving just ourselves) or more complex. Changes within organisations are typically complex and multi-dimensional, and to the people affected (positively or negatively) they often feel unbidden and are experienced as something that is happening to them rather than with them.

We have probably all experienced change that has gone awry in some aspect or other, often because commitment to change started to flag. This can be for numerous reasons. For instance, the original catalyst for change might have altered. This is common, in part because we generally don't have 20:20 vision when we embark on change but also because the pace of change is increasing and the environment in which we operate rarely stands still while we try to catch up. Less forgivable is when we trip ourselves up because we've not paid enough attention to a barrier that we knew would get in our way. Large-scale change brought about through mergers and acquisitions activity seems to lend itself to this fault.

One company I worked with recognised that for a particular acquisition to be successful money would need to be spent on upgrading and integrating the two CRM systems and cross-training the sales teams. The unified sales team would be better able to realise the cross-selling opportunities that had prompted the purchase in the first place.

However, somewhere down the line, the budget for this investment got cut, with the consequence that the two sales teams remained two sales teams, skilled only in their original areas of expertise. This might not have mattered but for the fact that the teams had been slimmed down (because the plan had been that the remaining team members would be multi-skilled), leaving the remaining sales people overwhelmed by the volume and complexity of work. In addition, the change programme had offered up the prospect for people to increase their capabilities and reward base. When this wasn't delivered, frustration replaced enthusiasm.

Take a moment to think about a change you've experienced at work:

Reflecting on change	
How were you affected?	
How did you react when you first heard about the change?	
What were some of the things you found difficult about the change?	
What were some of the things you enjoyed about it?	
How did people around you respond to the change?	
What helped you come to terms with the change?	
What one thing would you have done differently in handling the change? What difference would this have made?	

Little elephants grow into big elephants if they're not dealt with[36]

In another organisation I spoke with, their problem stemmed from a recent merger of two companies with very different cultures: one was conformist and process-driven and was great at winning low-margin business where efficiency was the driving factor; the other was more innovative and daring, willing to develop bespoke solutions to meet its customers' needs, and was great for complex customers who valued (and paid for) a high level of service and partnering.

The senior leaders involved in seeing through the merger knew the cultures were very different but paid little attention until they came perilously close to losing a long-standing, lucrative customer. In the gap between the two cultures a state of gross mistrust had developed, paralysing the very vibrancy that had been at the heart of the two companies' successes to date, and their ability to cooperate and act as one.

You would think that we would be used to change and would deal with it well – indeed it is a trait of human kind to be able to adapt. But that doesn't mean we don't have problems with it. Fortunately, our emotional response tends to occur in a certain pattern. There are a number of models for showing the stages we tend to go through[37]. The words that best describe the pattern to me form the acronym CICE: contentment (or complacency), ignore, confusion (or concern), enthusiasm. An example from a not-so-distant past shows how this works:

- **Content:** Not so many years ago, I was starting out in my first job as a political economist, and as the most junior member of the team I was landed with the early shift. Much to the amusement of my family, who know I don't do early mornings,

---

[36] A nod to the idiom "there's an elephant in the room", i.e. there is an obvious problem that people are aware of but don't want to talk about

[37] E.g. Elisabeth Kubler-Ross's 5-stages of grief model and Claes Janssen's 4 rooms of change model

this involved getting into the office every morning at 6.30am to cut up the stream of Reuters news wires that had come off the dot-matrix printer and file them into regional folders for the commissioning editor meeting at 8am. Apart from the early morning bit, I was okay with this: there was a certain satisfaction in seeing the news first.

- **Ignore:** Within a year, the internet was starting to make its way into our lives, but somehow it still seemed more efficient for one person (the office junior) to be doing this early morning sifting, and we continued with this pattern for at least another 12 months (though I'm glad to say it wasn't me doing it any longer).

- **Confusion/concern:** When it finally became apparent that the internet was here to stay, and we started to move to a process where each editor did their own searches, this felt disastrous to some people. One editor was seriously in danger of being buried underneath the piles of paper he had collected over the years from the dot matrix printer and hated the thought of not having these in future.

- **Enthusiasm:** Six months on from making the change, and we were revelling in all the things the new technology allowed us to do. It both expanded our reach as analysts (I could sit at my desk in Oxford and quickly find out what the change in gold price meant for the economy in Papua New Guinea) and put us each individually in control of what we wanted to focus on. It had expanded our capability and control.

In the scheme of things, this was a small but significant change that happened to many people of my generation. My father, a diplomat, never got beyond ignoring this technological shift, resolutely placing his new PC under his desk, safely out of the way. In contrast, my grandson knew how to Skype before he could talk and would probably shake his head in disbelief at the thought of a pre-internet age. His challenges will be different, but the pattern he will experience will be the same: CICE.

Understanding that this pattern of response exists is the first step. We also need to be aware of a few other things if we are going to lead people through change successfully:

- **What does it mean for me?** When change is first presented the first question anyone will have for you is: "what does this mean for me"? Be prepared to answer it – even if it is to say you don't yet know. It is very difficult to listen to the detail of a proposed change and engage positively with it if you're still waiting for the answer to this first question.

- **We go through all the stages of CICE:** Acknowledge that we go through phases as we respond to a change that is happening – whether it is something we've initiated or has been imposed on us.

- **We are likely to be at different stages in our response cycle:** Understand as a leader in a business, i.e. someone that has possibly introduced the change, that you might be experiencing the change in a different way to someone who has just found out about it: you might be feeling enthusiastic about the change 12 months after setting it going, forgetting the angst that it initially caused you and that someone else is currently struggling with. We also need to be aware that the phases people go through in responding to change are not linear: people may feel ecstatic about change one moment and despondent about it the next. We're human and complex. We can help people experiencing these swings by recognising them and being consistent in our picture of the future, giving them something to focus on.

- **Accelerate the path to enthusiasm:** As a manager or leader in the business we can help to shorten the time people spend in a state of complacency or angst, and bring them to a place where they can be enthusiastic. We do this by being as clear as possible about the need for change and where we're going, and involving people in shaping and delivering the change.

This last point is particularly important. By involving people (i.e. giving people freedom and encouragement to apply their skills), people feel part of the change and we automatically start to get buy-in because they are influencing what that change looks like.

If you have some changes coming up that you'll be going through with your team, take a few minutes to think about the following:

Engaging people through change	
How will the change affect your team?	
How will you explain the need for change?	
What concerns are your team likely to have?	
Why are you enthusiastic about the change?	
What are the things that you're avoiding mentioning – the elephants in the room – and how are you going to deal with them?	

All of these questions can also be put to your team once you have set the overall context; indeed, they offer a really good way to engage them in the process of change. However, in my experience, your team will expect you to have your own views on these issues, even if you acknowledge that they are incomplete.

What else do we need to do to engage people through change beyond being aware of the emotional effect it can have?

There are plenty of books on change, describing various methodologies. One of the most well known authors on the subject is John Kotter, who describes an 8-stage process[38]. From my own experience, and because my mind mainly works in threes, I've grouped the various stages into:

1. **Know:**
   - Where are you today and where you want to go
   - Know what you need to do to get there

2. **Act:**
   - Draw up your plans
   - Understand what success looks like
   - Turn the plans into action
   - Follow through with rigour and momentum

3. **Review:**
   - Check what worked and what didn't and adapt
   - Check where you have got to
   - Check that the destination is still valid
   - Take a new bearing on your destination
   - Celebrate your progress

---

[38] JP Kotter, *"Leading Change"*, 1996, and JP Kotter & H Rathgeber, *"Our Iceberg Is Melting: Changing and Succeeding Under Any Conditions"*, 2006

There are clear similarities with the Connecting People process: plot the journey, connect with people and involve people.

Knowing where you are and where you're going closely follows the steps described in the first of these, while the process of change offers us copious opportunities to connect with people and involve them. Indeed, you generally can't implement change without involving others; if you don't do this, you will fail to create followers, and will remain the 'lone nut'[39]. We have probably all had our 'lone nut' moments – they are deeply frustrating[40].

Advocating advocates

I have seen good use of advocate groups in a number of organisations and have personal experience of being part of such a group following up on actions triggered by an employee survey. Advocates lend authenticity and common sense to this traditional approach to engagement.

Advocates are particularly important in the context of change. One company I researched provides a useful example of how advocates can speed up the process of engaging people in a new reality. The journey for this company was not without pain, with workers affected by unexpected job-losses and restructuring following a buyout by a rival company that had a different business model and cultural ethos. This was followed by a further change in identity as the purchaser reorganised and rebranded.

However, the purchased company had always had a strong ethos of involving its workers, and leaders in the business made use of

---

[39] Derek Sivers "First Followers: Leadership lessons from dancing guy" – a must-see YouTube clip: https://www.youtube.com/watch?v=fW8amMCVAJQ

[40] One of my own lone nut moments came when I was trying to bring in some key account management practices in one of the organisations I worked for: until I started building consensus with other leaders across the business, my ideas sat gathering dust in glorious isolation.

this tradition as they set about the task of establishing what the future looked like and bringing people with them.

The extended leadership team took time to create a new vision, and review and reattach to their values. Crucially, they then got everyone else involved through a series of road-show events, where people were asked: "what would you do if you were the boss?" Employees from across the business came up with a lot of pertinent and practical suggestions, and a strong community of advocates emerged who were encouraged to own these ideas and put them into practice. By ceding control and facilitating this process, the leadership team had helped their employees feel part of the change and enthusiastic about their new reality and the future.

Of course it was not as easy as this makes it sound. Take up in this process was strong but not universal. Moreover, because the change was essentially behavioural in nature (i.e. for people to take and exercise ownership), leaders soon realised they needed to keep supporting people through the process: the launch couldn't by itself provide sufficient momentum to keep the changes going. Changes like this are complex and take time and energy.

The previous chapters offer a number of techniques that can be applied to the process of engaging people through change but there are also some specific techniques to highlight:

- As Kotter suggests in Stage 2 of his process for major change, create a **guiding coalition** with enough power and motivation to lead the change – these are the sponsors and champions of change and are the people who believe in and clearly see why change is needed and what change will bring. It may be the same people or a separate group, but I would also suggest that you need a highly effective **operational team** with the tenacity, rigour and skills to see the change through. This should include people from across the organisation that will influence (and be affected by) the success of the project. If this is a large-scale change (as in the case of *Advocating advocates* example), you could also consider creating an **advocate group** who act as a sounding board for the guiding coalition and operational team, and serve as enthusiasts for change, role-modelling the new behaviours and highlighting the opportunities that change might bring. These groups are good examples of how we can **involve people**.

- If it is a large-scale change you might want to consider setting out with a **pilot version**. This reduces the risk and allows you to learn; it also starts to provide you with success stories, which are essential as you start to get more people involved.

- Pay attention to the rugby ball model of engagement. For the change to be successful, you may need to reinterpret the **values** that guide your behaviours, or bring in a new **culture** and check whether your **processes** are supporting your new way of working or your old one. For instance, if you now need people to work more collaboratively, but continue to reward them for their individual contributions, don't be surprised if collaborative behaviours take a long time to blossom.

- As the change initiative rolls out, you will start talking to a wider audience across a range of media, which makes it more difficult to **communicate effectively and consistently** (see *Connect with people* and *Inspiring, trusted, authentic communicator of the 'why'*). You also need to be listening closely to feedback to pick up any **alarm bells** that might be ringing, telling you your plans are not going quite as expected. When (rather than if) you hear these, act quickly.

- **Celebrate progress, recognise and reward the contributions** people are making, and **demonstrate continuing commitment** to the changes.

While a lot of this is particularly relevant to large-scale change, smaller changes also need to be thought out. They may not require lots of people to guide and manage it, but don't underestimate the barriers or the need for good communications. The process of Know, Act, Review and the importance of bringing people with you are still relevant and important.

One thing you can guarantee when you embark on change: wherever you end up, it will be a different place from where you started. If you pay attention to the process, and in particular to taking people with you, you are more likely to end up close to where you thought you would. If you don't, your destination becomes far less certain.

Developing effective virtual teams

Picture a virtual team. What do you see: a group of people based in far-flung places, coalescing around laptops at some horribly early or late hour to accommodate time zones, bemoaning their internet connection speeds, to discuss, in a slightly fragmented way, something they are jointly developing or managing? These sorts of teams certainly exist in our increasingly globalised world. However, virtual teams can also involve people in the same country or even building.

A key distinction between a virtual and non-virtual team is proximity: people in the former typically don't sit next to each other in a conventional office; the latter typically do. Virtual teams also often comprise people who have diverse reporting lines and are working on a myriad other things at the same time. If we look at it like this, many of us spend a lot of our time working in virtual teams.

There are numerous lists on the web giving the top 5, 10, 20, 50 tips on how to manage virtual teams and arguing the case for and against people working remotely[41]. Let me cut through the argument to give you my stance on the issue of where people work, then I'll give you my

---

[41] In 2013 CEO Marissa Mayer banned Yahoo's 12,000 employees from working from home; *"Why Remote Workers Are More (Yes, More) Engaged"*, Scott Edinger, Harvard Business Review, 2012 offers an alternative perspective

own list of some things to think about that might help people engage with each other when working in virtual teams.

Stance first. There are of course no right or wrong answers about this. My general premise is that we should work wherever we are most productive. Behind that statement come a number of assumptions: we are adults and want to do a good, professional job, whatever that might be. In terms of control, it is pretty easy to see whether we are producing what we're asked to produce, to the quality desired. Given this, does it matter where I sit or what hours I work?

It depends on the task in hand. If I am writing a report on commercial risk in Finland (which, odd though it may sound, I sometimes do), the most important thing is that I can research the topic and then share my analysis, in written form, with my editors. I can do all this sat wherever I like as long as I have a connection to the internet. Indeed, I once managed an analyst who let me know he was filing his report from a beach in Australia… quite irritating when I was sitting in the UK in the midst of a damp British winter, but he was highly productive and did what I needed when I needed it.

Conversely, when I'm designing a customer management or engagement programme with a client, face-to-face conversations are vital: it is much quicker to generate ideas and check understanding when the person you are working with is physically in the same room as you are. And as for workshops… as an interactive experience, they really don't work in the virtual world (yet[42]). Tasks that require collaboration or a degree of innovation generally benefit from working in proximity with others, at least to get things going.

Thus the premise becomes: **we should work wherever we are most productive for the task in hand.**

---

[42] Dr. Nicola Millard has produced some interesting papers on this topic as part of her role with BT, including *"Establishing Common Ground for Collaboration in Virtual Organisations"*

We can do a quick sense check on this. In the example of the Australian freelancer given above, this worked for him but would not have worked for me (way too much sand and sun!). Equally, I know from experience that it was pretty difficult to do this sort of work in a noisy open-plan office. Next time you walk around your open-plan office, check how many people are wearing headphones: this is probably not because they are anti-social, but because the task they are working on requires a certain level of individual concentration that they would otherwise find hard to accommodate.

Does this premise - we should work wherever we are most productive for the task in hand - apply to a team?

The example given above about writing on Finland may look as though it is an individual task but the process of getting that analysis published involves a team. It looks individual because each member of the team has very defined roles in the process – it is a relay race that requires each individual to run their bit of the track and co-ordinate with the next person in the chain as the baton is handed over.

This team is skilled and practiced in what it does and the task lends itself to very clear, distinct and discrete activities. What happens when the task is less clear? For instance, at the start of a product development project we might have an idea that we want to develop a new product, but we are not quite sure what that looks like or how we'll market it, and we're working as a cross-functional team with people we've not worked with before.

A short exercise: imagine yourself as the project manager trying to get this new product off the ground.

First imagine what you would need to do if you can't get everyone in the same room:

- Does it involve a lot of phoning around, setting up conference calls (some offices have video, some don't; some people can use Skype on the their laptops, some can't)?

- As you canvass opinion about the product you're tasked with developing, how do you account for the different opinions you are getting in each conversation and how do you relay them to the rest of the group?
- Is there a sense of shared ownership and purpose of task?

Now imagine getting everyone together in a room for two days, setting out the overall aim, sharing your ideas, planning how to bring those ideas to life, allocating/volunteering to head up certain tasks, splitting out the work for sub-groups to pursue, reconvening at a given point to check progress...

How do the two versions feel to you?

It is likely that the second scenario felt easier. It is still not without its obstacles, but you've potentially got rid of a lot of them in that first meeting.

Of course it is not always possible to get people together to work on things that would benefit from proximity. This is where the list comes in. I've concentrated on the things that I think help people to feel part of a team and engage fully in the task in hand:

- Work out how you're going to communicate and then be disciplined and rigorous about doing it
- Build relationships and nurture trust
- Have the right people in the team
- Spend time with people individually
- Get together
- Your role in connecting people

Work out how you're going to communicate and then be disciplined and rigorous about doing it

Everyone in the team will need to be disciplined and conscious of how you are communicating given that you are missing a lot of the clues that you might get from seeing each other in the office. Consider the various forms of communication activities – information sharing, idea-creation, decision-making, social interaction – and what technologies will help you most with each of them. For example:

- Instant messaging systems such as Chatter, Yammer, Skype etc. are great for conversations, or quick updates and questions. The team at Planet K2 use Skype in exactly this way.

- Emails are good tools for information sharing (from one person to many) but can get messy and frustrating if you're using them to have a conversation with more than 2 or 3 people.

- Phone calls or conference calls (preferably with video) can work well for team catch-ups, but make sure you apply the normal rules for effective meetings with additional rigor (e.g. circulate the agenda before the meeting to give people time to prepare, have clear roles and expectations for people in the meeting, be disciplined about time, make sure people are not talking over each other and that everyone has the opportunity to contribute).

- When you are scheduling calls, be sensitive to time-zone challenges. One US-UK team I worked with had the unfortunate habit of scheduling all meetings for mid-day/afternoon in the US, meaning their UK colleagues always had late afternoon or evening calls, making for very long days and disrupted home lives; the UK team still came in to the office at 8 o'clock every morning, literally to do their day jobs. Over the months this eroded people's willingness to engage and weakened the team's effectiveness.

- Use share spaces (e.g. Dropbox, SharePoint, etc.) for documents, update bulletins, resources and project trackers.

Don't assume you or others know how to use all these technology platforms. It is worth spending some time getting up to speed on the basics and involving the team on sharing usage tips that make you more effective (warning: it is very easy to spend lots of time on gadgets that don't actually make you more productive!).

Once you've got to grips with the software and hardware, also check the behaviours. Like people in an office, people working remotely will have different preferences for chattiness and sharing information. It is worth acknowledging this and setting some expectations at the start.

You may also need to spend some time helping people to change ingrained habits if they're preventing them from working effectively in a virtual environment. For instance, if someone is used to mulling over their ideas verbally as they pop into their head, they might get frustrated working in a team where time zones make it difficult to just call someone up; they might need to consider ways of capturing their thoughts and going through them at a more mutually convenient time. It will take conscious effort and a period of time to make such an adjustment (months rather than days).

Build relationships and nurture trust

People working in teams, collaborating, need to be able to trust each other, at least to the degree that you are sure people on the team are doing what they say they will do, in a competent, reliable way.

The normal rules apply but with a virtual team you may need to be more conscious and directive, e.g.:

- Be clear (i.e. check everyone has the same understanding) about the functional roles and responsibilities people have in the team.
- Acknowledge and make use of different team behavioural roles: some are doers, some directors, some provide the social glue, some provide the disharmony and left-field thinking. All are valuable.

- Consider the needs of each individual and how you can provide an environment that encourages them to participate fully. For example, you could ask a task-oriented person to track the project and report on progress; or involve highly collaborative people in organising the team meetings and sharing information.

- Consider how you will both encourage and manage disharmony or conflict in the team. This could include being overt about areas of disagreement, having separate conversations with individuals where positions appear entrenched (but beware of isolating people – this can feel like being bullied), and working out how your team will conclude disagreements and move on – it is difficult to shake hands across continents!

Have the right people on the right team

I'm always a bit wary of prescribing the sort of competences people *should* have. These can either end up being very long lists that essentially describe super-men and women, or risk perpetuating cloning: that person is really good in this role, and these are their competencies, therefore we should recruit more people like that. One of the essential qualities of a team is that it enables you to bring in people with different approaches, skills and competencies, and the sum becomes stronger than the parts. If we want to preserve this quality, we want people in our team who have a variety of complementary attributes.

That said, I'll risk a small list of things you might look for when choosing people to work on a virtual team. First and foremost, you are looking for people who behave like adults, i.e. they will solve their own problems if they can, ask for help when they need it, and don't wait to be rescued. They probably also have a high quotient of the things we see in highly engaged people: they collaborate, persevere, take ownership and responsibility, are curious and want to improve (see *How do engaged and disengaged people behave?*).

Spend time with people individually

Depending on the task, timeline and people this might be a one-to-one catch-up call once a day, once a week or once a month, using a video link if possible; also make sure that you meet face-to-face occasionally. Project work might drive the agenda for these calls but also give time to an open agenda for that person to fill (proper time, not two minutes squeezed in at the end). Ask "how are things going for you?" or "what has stood out for you since we last talked about this?" and then dial up your listening skills. You may not have the luxury of seeing the person you are talking with (and video links have their limitations) so your auditory skills need to be as good as you can get them. CALIBRE listening offers some pointers (see *Developer of people*):

- Concentrate: listen to the words, the tone and the pauses, listen for what's not being said
- Acknowledge what's being said
- Leave room for silence – this is quite tricky on the phone but important
- Show interest - again this more difficult when you're not sat with someone. As your body language can't necessarily be seen, you need to show interest by paying attention and picking up on what's being said.
- Be in the room (or on the call!): get rid of distractions and clear your mind
- Response: suggest options based on what you've heard and listen to the answer before thinking of the next question
- Evaluate: be aware of your own judgement filters and tone them down.

Get together

Having said it is not always possible to get people together, it is still important to do so, particularly at the start of a new project, but also fairly regularly thereafter (e.g. twice a year for a long-standing team; more frequently, particularly at first, for a new or temporary team). Use the time well – both to cover the task in hand and to build the human and social bonds that form the basis of trust. Involve the team in working out what works for them – fishing trips against a backdrop of snow-tipped Chilean volcanoes seemed to hit the mark for a team my husband worked with, though I swear the photos each year showed the same fish!

Your role in connecting people

As a leader in this team, your role is to help the people in it function really effectively by doing all the things listed above: structuring, engaging, facilitating. If we were to sum this up it would be about being a master connector of people.

A short exercise for people who manage virtual teams. Consider the following (you might want to check your perceptions with some members of the team):

Managing a virtual team	
How good are we at accommodating and making use of each other's styles? How could we be even better at this?	
How clear are our communications? How could we be even better at this?	

How attached are we feeling to the overall purpose of the team? How could we increase this?	
What is the one thing we could do that would help us to be even more effective than we are currently? What's stopping us from doing this? How do we get that obstacle out of the way?	

Building profitable, long-lasting customer relationships

Right at the start of this book I pointed to the Engage for Success study showing a strong correlation between high levels of engagement and increased customer satisfaction (see *Why bother?*)[43]. When we consider the attributes of highly engaged people – they are capable, they own things, they persevere, they're curious, they collaborate (see *How do engaged and disengaged people behave?*) – it is hardly surprising that customers are more satisfied. Engaged, capable people who have the freedom to operate get things done; as a customer, this is exactly what I want.

---

[43] Also see: H Qiu & EK Macdonald, "Improving customer experience through employee engagement: a new take on the service-profit chain framework", Cranfield Customer Management Forum, Cranfield School of Management

By way of an illustration, I was recently going through the process of setting up a new bank account. For much of the time, this was a painful experience. I felt as though I was dealing with people who didn't appreciate what I was trying to do and were constrained by following a tick-box checklist set of questions. However, just as I was about to lose my patience and go elsewhere, I encountered an entirely different attitude: here was someone who clearly had the same checklist and remit, but she went out of her way to understand my problem and was helpful in her suggestions of how to resolve it. It felt like night and day. Same bank, same procedures, different attitude.

This leads us to a fairly obvious conclusion: as managers and leaders in a business we need to recruit and nurture highly engaged people in customer-facing roles.

Of course, this becomes a bit more challenging when we realise that most (possibly all) roles in our organisations in someway touch the customer. The link is most obvious for our sales and customer service teams, but our customers are also affected by our HR policies and who we hire, by people in finance, who structure the deals and are often involved in pricing or costing decisions, by the delivery teams who make sure the customer gets what they signed up for and so on. Ideally we want to recruit the right people into all roles. But if this all feels a bit too much of a mountain to climb, break it down and choose a place to start.

One of the things I specialise in as an engagement practitioner is helping my clients build their key account management capabilities. This has various merits as a place to start beyond it being a specialism of mine. Your key accounts are, by definition, the ones that make a significant difference to your business. It would therefore make sense to employ your most capable, engaged people in the teams that look after and grow these accounts.

By their nature these accounts tend also to require a more complex response from us. These customers are not buying widgets at the lowest price; they want us to help them be successful and this is not something they can get from an automated order system on the internet. This is where the whole engagement process comes in:

- **Plot the journey:** This is about analysing where you and your customer are, then working out where they want to get to and how you can help them (to mutual gain!).

- **Connecting people:** Collaboration – internally and externally - is crucial to effective customer management. The commercial owner of the account is now often routinely supported by specialists and after-sales support and it is likely that this team is interacting with more than one person in the buyer organisation. Everyone involved needs to understand – and care about - what you're jointly looking to achieve.

- **Involve people:** Create the framework and guidelines that allow and encourage people to contribute fully to the success of the customer relationship.

Of course, using this process – plot, connect, involve - effectively is more difficult when applied to a customer. It can be hard enough getting the rugby ball (see Figure 4) aligned within one organisation, let alone across two. Again, break the task down and focus on what your account team and the purchasing team are looking to achieve. Believe me, if you are successful in this, your organisation will want to know how you're doing what you're doing and extend it out more widely.

A short exercise for people managing customer teams (which of course is everyone). Consider the following (you might want to check some of your perceptions with others in the team and the customer organisation):

Managing a customer team	
How clear is everyone in the team about what your customer and your own organisation are looking to achieve?	
How clear is everyone about how you are planning to achieve this outcome?	
How clear are people about their roles on the team? What are people confident about? How can you help them to keep this topped up? What are they uncertain about? How can you help them reduce this?	
What do you need to do as a team to be even more effective in keeping and growing your customer?	

Just in case you are thinking this is all about big business and big customers, my final story of passionate customer engagement comes from a small business, The Real Food Café at Tyndrum in Scotland[44]. It sells fish and chips... really good fish and chips (it was winner of the national Fish & Chips Awards in 2013 and 2014). Its values and way of

---

[44] Information gleaned from visits and the Real Food Café leaflets and website www.therealfoodcafecom

working used to be up on the walls for people to see, but actually this wasn't necessary: every customer going in for a much-needed break and refreshment gets to experience what the place is about. Could the same be said for your customers? What do they experience when they buy from you?

Overlaying the Connecting People process we can see it's all there at the Real Food Café:

- **Plot the journey:** They are really clear on what they do and why they do it.

- **They provide:** *"Locally sourced and homemade snack meals at reasonable prices in a relaxed environment."*

- **And know why they do it:** *"We are working with great pride and determination to give you, our customers, a splendid taste of our unique Scottish hospitality. In doing this, we are creating an iconic café serving real local food with a sustained vigour both now and in future years working hand in hand with the community. Get on board! Be part of it!"*

- **Connect with people:** Their 'Rules of the Game' are all about service and getting involved, both as employees and as people working in a local community. These 'rules of the game' are highly visible in what people working in the café actually do:

    ☐ *"Get to know the customers, talk to them as guests*

    ☐ Take time to listen

    ☐ Get involved with the community

    ☐ Ask for help"

- **Involve people:** It is clear when you go into the café that everyone working there is part of a team. They know what they are doing, why they are doing it and they actively work on creating an engaging environment. This is beautifully summed up in my favourite 'rules of the game' about attitude:

"We choose to adopt a positive outlook and energy at work."

I'm sure there are days when the person working their way through another ton of potatoes or frying yet another piece of haddock would rather be climbing high above in the mountains and finds it difficult to smile at the next customer. But somehow, they always do.

11

What do you do next?

Connecting People has hopefully given you some ideas about how you could go about creating and maintaining environments where people are fully engaged, contributing and participating to the full extent of their ever-expanding abilities. Practise, be enthusiastic and enjoy watching the environment you create grow.

Appendix: Case Studies

The case studies were compiled through a mixture of interviews, general research and direct experience. I also interviewed people who wanted to contribute but didn't want their views to be directly attributable. Their insights and experiences have been woven into the book as appropriate.

Advocating advocates

I have seen good use of advocate groups in a number of organisations and have personal experience of being part of such a group following up on actions triggered by an employee survey. Advocates lend authenticity and common sense to this traditional approach to engagement.

Advocates are particularly important in the context of change. One company I researched provides a useful example of how advocates can speed up the process of engaging people in a new reality. The journey for this company was not without pain, with workers affected by unexpected job-losses and restructuring following a buyout by a rival company that had a different business model and cultural ethos. This was followed by a further change in identity as the purchaser reorganised and rebranded. However, the purchased company had always had a strong ethos of involving its workers, and leaders in the business made use of this tradition as they set about the task of establishing what the future looked like and bringing people with them.

The extended leadership team took time to create a new vision, and review and reattach to their values. Crucially, they then got everyone else involved through a series of road-show events, where people were asked: "what would you do if you were the boss?" Employees from across the business came up with a lot of pertinent and practical suggestions, and a strong community of advocates emerged who were encouraged to own these ideas and put them into practice. By ceding control and facilitating this process, the leadership team had helped their employees feel part of the change and enthusiastic about their new reality and the future.

Of course it was not as easy as this makes it sound. Take up in this process was strong but not universal. Moreover, because the change was essentially behavioural in nature (i.e. for people to take and exercise ownership), leaders soon realised they needed to keep supporting people through the process: the launch couldn't by itself provide sufficient momentum to keep the changes going. Changes like this are complex and take time and energy.

D&B

Dun & Bradstreet set out on 20th July 1841 to provide information on businesses with a view to helping them trade on the right terms. This remains their core purpose, but the manner in which they do this has changed dramatically. Some of the changes have been imposed on the company (it is difficult to keep pace in the digital age and explosion of data) but D&B has also frequently been at the forefront of technological advances: putting in one of the first mass orders for typewriters to equip its reporters, through to developing a unique classification system to allow a single view of a customer to be established (a requirement that sits at the centre of much of the new regulation surrounding banks). Technology advancements have changed both how D&B goes about its business and the scope of its business. Both of these dynamics need to be understood and explained to customers and employees alike.

Danone Baby Nutrition (UK)

Danone is a large, multinational company with a string of best-selling consumer brands. However, while they are a big company with over 100,000 employees world-wide, they have adopted a business model that gives local business units considerable autonomy to build and drive their parts of the organisation as they see fit. People are given a clear purpose, framework and expectation, and are then given the freedom to use their strengths to good effect. HR Director Liz Ellis puts some of their success down to the size of the business unit (~250 people), which allows people to remain in touch with each other and come together around a defined purpose. People maintain personal connections; they can see what they are responsible for as a team and individually, and can see the direct effects.

Teamwork is crucial to this business, as is the emphasis on using strengths and being dissatisfied with the status quo (individuals and teams regularly use the Stop, Start, Do Differently technique). Their appraisal system affords behaviours as much weight as outcomes, as does their reward and recognition scheme 'Do You Dare To Dream', which has helped to develop a culture of people 'dreaming the impossible stuff', and applying it to both their personal lives and their work.

When I asked Liz what her advice would be to other organisations keen on developing an environment where high engagement is the norm she offered three suggestions:

1. Have daily, one-to-one interactions with people.
2. Find a way to get the business to take engagement seriously.
3. Continue to nurture: e.g. by calling out behaviours that are not helpful; by giving feedback; by having safe havens where people can let off steam and regroup.

Kier Group plc

When I spoke with Kier's Customer Experience Director, Jackie Ducker, we pretty quickly agreed that engaged employees are the key to delighting customers, and our conversation rapidly moved to exploring how that happens and where to start.

For Kier, it started with their customers telling them they were confused about what the company did. When they asked the people who worked for Kier 'what do you do?', customers would be told: we build hospitals OR we mend roads OR we build houses.... This came across as inconsistent and parochial, and risked customers looking for other suppliers because they didn't know how Kier could help them. In contrast, the breadth of the new vision makes it clear that Kier offers many things to many people – customers and employees alike. The statement describing what Kier does ("invests in, builds, maintains and renews the places where we live, work and play") is relevant to all.

For Jackie, getting this vision right – and securing leadership commitment to it – was the essential first step. But as she said "the words are meaningless until they become embedded and are made real". To start this off, Kier listened to insights from its customers and employees, and followed this up with 100 people coming together from across the organisation to work out what Kier looked and felt like when it was at its best. The words that resonated most, and that people felt made the greatest difference to customers and themselves, were 'enthusiastic, collaborative and forward thinking'. It is by showing enthusiasm, working collaboratively, and thinking ahead that the people in Kier intend to realise its vision: "To be a world-class, customer-focused company that invests in, builds, maintains and renews the places where we live, work and play".

Having established the narrative of the company's vision and how it will be achieved, Kier is now in the throes of bringing the words to life and embedding them in the fabric of the organisation. At the time of writing, this is still work-in-progress. A series of road shows are being held to introduce the vision around the company and provide employees with an opportunity to understand and feel excited about how they can help make it happen. In addition, cross-functional teams are being set up to look at the every-day, operational activities of the business and ensure they support (and don't hinder!) enthusiastic, collaborative, forward-thinking ways of working.

Using cross-functional teams in this way has many benefits. They bring together expertise and different points of view from across organisations, ensuring richer outcomes and helping to bridge any siloes that might exist. Members of these teams also become advocates for, and role models of, the changes that are occurring, encouraging others to follow. And of course, multiple teams allow the tasks to be parcelled out in manageable lots, making the whole process less vulnerable to fatigue.

Little elephants grow into big elephants if they're not dealt with

In another organisation I spoke with, their problem stemmed from a recent merger of two companies with very different cultures: one was conformist and process-driven and was great at winning low-margin business where efficiency was the driving factor; the other was more innovative and daring, willing to develop bespoke solutions to meet its customers' needs, and was great for complex customers who valued (and paid for) a high level of service and partnering.

The senior leaders involved in seeing through the merger knew the cultures were very different but paid little attention until they came perilously close to losing a long-standing, lucrative customer. In the gap between the two cultures a state of gross mistrust had developed, paralysing the very vibrancy that had been at the heart of the two companies' successes to date, and their ability to cooperate and act as one.

Passing on your company DNA

Operating in the fast-moving world of technology, this company has grown exponentially in little more than a decade from an idea to a medium-sized, international company employing over 500 people. The tipping point for the company came in 2012-13, when they reached the 250-employee mark. The company realised that the rapid pace of expansion in staff numbers was putting the company's DNA at risk, with the new recruits (many at a senior level) diluting not only what had made the company successful so far, but what the executive team also saw as being important for them in the future.

With this realisation, the company invested time and money in their on-boarding process, allowing people to experience, assimilate and align with the company's DNA. Indeed, when I interviewed a senior director at the company and asked what his one piece of advice would be for other companies, it was to "get the on-boarding right, but understand it takes time and it takes longer than you think." Key to this process was to ensure that everyone in the organisation (the people going through the on-boarding process, their colleagues, their managers) understood the process and had the right expectations: "Give people time to take everything on board and then they will be productive in the way you recognise; leaders must avoid being too impatient to get to this point."

Shire

The pioneering pharmaceutical company Shire is all about purpose. The company exists to be 'brave'. This one word represents their business model, the people they help and their staff: they develop niche medical interventions that help people with life-changing, often rare, illnesses, and make brave decisions that push the boundaries of what was previously considered possible. Brave might also be applied to their growth plans. After a failed takeover by AbbVie in 2014, Shire's purchase of NPS in 2015 reaffirms its independence and bravery: while NPS clearly fits the Shire profile (it has two rare disease products), it didn't make a profit during 30-years in business.

The Mid-Staffordshire NHS Foundation Trust

'Cautionary tale' makes it sound as though this comes from the fairy stories of the Brothers Grimm. Unfortunately, this tale is very real and relates to the catastrophic events that put the Stafford Hospital and the Mid-Staffordshire NHS Foundation Trust into the headlines for all the wrong reasons, with people dying who shouldn't have.

- *NHS hospital scandal which left 1,200 dead could happen again, warn campaigners - Daily Mail*
- *NHS trust's litany of failure, neglect, insensitivity and ineptitude - The Guardian*
- *Hospital condemned over deaths after 'appalling' failures in care - The Guardian*

An easy conclusion to jump to was that the culture in the NHS had gone wrong; that somehow the staff had stopped caring for their patients. Professor David Buchanan, Professor Mike Bourne and Steve Macaulay of Cranfield University looked into this and came to a different conclusion. Their research showed that people working in the NHS were strongly motivated and wanted to make a difference for patients, deliver innovation and change, do a good job, feel valued, and develop others - all characteristics of highly engaged people (see *How do engaged and disengaged people behave?*).

However, these motivations were stifled by an autocratic, unsupportive, top-down management style, a complex regulatory regime, constant change in structures (requiring people to spend a lot of energy forging new relationships and understand changes in their role), metrics that focussed too narrowly on financial performance and seemed to ignore the 'softer' measures around care, and a significant cost reduction programme. The will was there but the environment wasn't.

Appendix: MAP tool

Goal/event:		
	What are you going to do?	How are you going to do it?
Must		
Aspire		
Phenomenal		

How to use the MAP tool:

- Consider *what* you must do to achieve a successful outcome (make these actions SMART – specific, measureable, achievable, relevant, time-bound), and *how* you're going to do it (e.g. what strengths are you going to use to achieve these things). Check: you cannot achieve your goal or consider the event a success without these things.

- Consider what you aspire to do, and how you're going to achieve it. Check: you would feel proud if you achieved this.

- Consider what would be truly phenomenal if you achieved it, and how you're going to do it.

- Finally, review your must – you might find it looks or feels too conservative. If it does, go for something more ambitious!

Appendix: HIC tool– Help, Impact, Control

Help

A: Make use of it if an easy opportunity arises

B: Don't spend energy looking to use this

Low impact

E: Be aware of it but don't spend energy fixing it

F: Fix it if you've got time; low priority

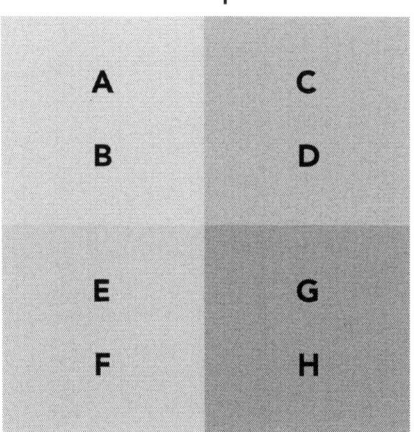

	A	C	
	B	D	
	E	G	
	F	H	

C: Make use of this

D: Gain influence or control of this and use it

High impact

G: Gain influence or control over this to minimise the impact

H: Fix it

Hinder

How to use the HIC tool:

- Establish the goal you want to achieve.

- What activities, factors in the environment, behaviours will either help or hinder you in achieving this goal? Put each item on a sticky note.

- Place each note along the horizontal axis (help above the line, hinder below) according to how much impact it will have.
- Now move the notes vertically according to how much control you have over it.
- Consider what actions you need to take over each action and prioritise.

Appendix: Gap Analysis

This tool was developed by my BRAC colleague Sabina Mangosi. Process:

- Identify your success factors: these are the things that are going to help you, your team and/or your organisation be successful in your desired future state. You might want to consider what your competitors are doing, what leading lights in other industries are doing, how buying patterns are changing, what opportunities new technologies might bring etc.

- Decide how important each one is (its weighting): assign each factor with a weighting of between 1 and 100, with the total adding up to 100.

- Assess how good you are at these things now (current level): assign a score of 1.0 for high, 0.5 for medium and 0.0 for low.

- Calculate the score: current level x weighting. Add up to find the total.

- Consider what the optimal level might be in 3-5 years time (this might not be 100).

- The difference between where you are now and the optimal level is the gap you need to solve through development of your existing staff or recruitment of people with these particular attributes.

Success Factor, e.g.	Current level[1]	Weighting	Score[2]
Sales leadership	0.5	25	12.5
New business acquisition	0.0	15	0
Training	0.5	10	5
Internal collaboration	0.5	20	10
Solution development	0.0	10	0
Agility	0.0	20	0
Total		**100**	**27.5**

[1]*High=1.0; Medium=0.5; Low=0.0*
[2]*The closer the total is to 100 the better*

Presenting this in a chart across a given time span helps to make the point about the effort that's going to be required to get to your desired state. Often the chart shows a dip to start with: when you set out to do things differently, you may find you get worse before you get better.

Reading list

TM Amabile & SJ Kramer, *"The Power of Small Wins"*, Harvard Business Review, May 2011

R Bolton & D Grover Bolton, *"Social Style/Management Style: developing productive work relationships"*, 1984

R Bolton & D Grover Bolton *"People styles at work and beyond"*, 2nd edition, 2009

T R Clark, *"The Employee Engagement Mindset: the six drivers for tapping into the hidden potential of everyone in your company"*, 2012

S Cranston & S Keller, *"Increasing the 'meaning quotient' of work"*, McKinsey Quarterly, Jan 2013

M Csikszentmihalyi, *"Flow: the classic work on how to achieve happiness"*, 2002

K Hatter, C Shambrook, J Constable, K Grainger, *"Perform"*, Dec 2013

G Johnson, R Whittington, K Scholes, *"Fundamentals of Strategy"*, Pearson Education, 2012

G Johnson & K Scholes *"Exploring Corporate Strategy"*, 1993

S Knight, *"NLP at work: the essence of excellence"*, 2009

JP Kotter, *"Leading Change"*, 1996

JP Kotter & H Rathgeber, *"Our Iceberg Is Melting: Changing and Succeeding Under Any Conditions"*, 2006

P Lencioni, *"The five dysfunctions of a team: a leadership fable"*, 2002 and *"Overcoming the five dysfunctions of a team"*, 2005

N Millard *"Establishing Common Ground for Collaboration in Virtual Organisations"*, BT white paper

ME Porter, *"The five competitive forces that shape strategy"*, Harvard Business Review, Jan 2008

H Qiu & EK Macdonald, *"Improving customer experience through employee engagement: a new take on the service-profit chain framework"*, Cranfield Customer Management Forum, Cranfield School of Management

C Taylor, *"Walking the Talk: building a culture for success"*, 2005

J Whitmore, *"Coaching for Performance" GROWing human potential and purpose"*, 2009

C Wilson, *"Performance Coaching: a complete guide to best practice coaching and training"*, 2014

A bit about Kate Davies

Kate's operational background and familiarity with running large teams, budgets and change programmes lends authenticity to the work she has done in developing highly engaged teams across all areas of a business. Her academic and analytical knowledge lends further rigour to this practical experience: she is an associate fellow at the University of Cranfield's School of Management and holds a business degree and a masters in international relations.

Motivated by the conviction that people with high levels of engagement make it possible for businesses to achieve outstanding results, Kate works with a number of organisations to equip people, teams and businesses to engage with each other, particularly during periods of change. She believes that if you get this right, consistent, outstanding effort by the individual and the team becomes the default rather than being discretionary – that's when an organisation, and the people in it, truly grows.

You can find out more about Kate, the people she works with, and her vintage tractor, at www.lecconnect.co.uk and uk.linkedin.com/in/equippingpeopletoengage/en